ALL-TIME FAVORITE CARD GAMES

David Galt

PUBLICATIONS INTERNATIONAL, LTD.

David Galt is a game designer and consultant who has written extensively on games old and new. His articles have appeared in *Games* magazine, *The Playing Card,* and *Country Collectibles,* and he is also the author of *Card Games for One or Two.* His collection of over 5000 antique games and playing cards includes some of the first in America.

Cover illustration: Guy Wolek

CONTENTS

IT'S IN THE CARDS

Can you keep a poker face and play it close to the vest? Well then, here's a not-so-well-kept secret: For the past 600 years, card games have been a great way for people of all ages to have fun!

Card games bring people together to have fun—that's why they've been around so long. Just listen to the words we use, and you'll hear plenty of everyday phrases that stem from the world of card playing.

A veteran Euchre player, for instance, knows the right time to "play a lone hand." "That goes double in spades" is often heard at Pinochle and Gin Rummy tables. Winners at Poker tend to have an "ace in the hole." In Solo, Setback, and Bézique, you must know when to "play your trump card."

Besides encouraging communication, cards teach us a lot. Children can learn about numbers through games like Crazy Eights, Fan Tan, and War. Casino, Cribbage, and Michigan are among the many games that show us the factor of luck. Spades and I Doubt It require sneaky tactics and a certain amount of guesswork.

 Learn how to play these games and more! The following pages provide instructions for 29 of the most popular card games of all time. For each game, you will find rules of play, game objective, suggested number of players, card requirements, and scoring rules. Also included are tips to help you formulate a strategy, as well as variations for modifying each game. The rules provided are merely guidelines; you may develop your own variations as well. The handy glossary should be useful for defining important terms.

So, if you're looking for fun, look through this book. You're sure to find a card game to suit any occasion!

AUCTION PINOCHLE

Although Pinochle developed in Europe out of the popular game Bézique, Auction Pinochle probably was invented by immigrants to America. Its appeal was greatest a century ago, and many believe it to be the all-time-best three-handed card game.

Number of players: Three (or four, with the dealer sitting out each deal).

Object: To score points in melds and in play.

The cards: A 48-card "Pinochle" pack is used. You can put one together from two standard packs by dropping all deuces through 8s. Cards rank—from high to low—A-10-K-Q-J-9.

To play: Deal 15 cards to each player. By tradition, deal in bunches of three, or one bunch of three followed by bunches of four. Deal three cards (not the last three) to a face-down "widow," or "kitty."

The bidding: Starting with the player at dealer's left, each player bids or passes. The lowest bid is 250 points, and bids increase by ten points thereafter. Once you pass you can't reenter the bidding, but bidders can continue raising the auction. The auction is closed once two players have passed. The aim is to score at least as many points as you bid, by scoring for melds and winning tricks (see "Melds in Pinochle").

The player who wins the bid becomes the "bidder." If you are the bidder, turn the three widow cards face up and add them to your hand. It may be clear at this point that your total of melds and cards taken in play won't reach your bid. You may concede at this point, losing the amount you bid.

With this hand, a 300 bid is safe. You have "100 Aces" to meld, plus
pinochle (♠Q-♦J), and the "dix" of trumps, worth 10. In play, your
hand should take 150 points. You also have two flushes "open," and
if you get a lucky widow, you might have much more to meld. It's
probably best not to risk a 400 bid on this type of hand, though.

Melds in Pinochle:

Flush (A-10-K-Q-J of trumps)	150 points
Royal Marriage (K-Q of trumps)	40 points
Plain Marriage (K-Q of other suit)	20 points
Pinochle (♠Q-♦J)	40 points
100 Aces (♠A-♥A-♣A-♦A)	100 points
80 Kings (♠K-♥K-♣K-♦K)	80 points
60 Queens (♠Q-♥Q-♣Q-♦Q)	60 points
40 Jacks (♠J-♥J-♣J-♦J)	40 points
Dix (pronounced 'deece') (9 of trumps)	10 points

(If you declare a flush, you may not also declare the royal marriage
it contains.)

Otherwise, table your melds, including cards from the widow, and
announce a suit as trumps. If the bidder has already reached or
exceeded the value of his bid, play ceases immediately, and he
scores the value of his game (see "Scoring").

Your two opponents will temporarily unite in their play against
you. In order to reduce your hand back down to 15 cards, choose
three unmelded cards to set aside, face down, to add later to the
tricks you win. Pick up your melds, and lead any card to the first
trick.

The winner of each trick leads to the next. You must always follow suit, and if you cannot follow to a plain suit you must play a trump if possible. When a trump is led, play a higher trump than the previous player if possible. Tricks are taken by the highest card of the suit led or by the highest trump if they are played.

Your trumps.   Opponents' trumps.

You lead ♥K, so opponents must play ♥10 and ♥A. This allows you to win the remaining trumps when you regain the lead.

When two of the same card, say two ♠As, are played to a trick, the one played first is considered the higher of the two.

When play is over, points are counted in tricks as follows:

Ace	11	Queen	3
10	10	Jack	2
King	4	9	0

Last trick wins 10 points.

Scoring: If you make your bid, collect points from each opponent according to the following scoring table. If you concede, lose points to each opponent according to the scoring table. If you play the hand and miss your bid, lose double to each opponent for going bête (pronounced 'bait').

Bid	Points
250–290	5
300–340	10
350–390	15
400–440	25
450–490	50
500+	100

For bids over 300, spades score double.

Example: You bid 370, and make 405, in spades. You receive 30 points from each opponent. If you had bid 400 and made 405 in spades, you'd win 50 from each. But, if you'd bid 410 and made only 405, you'd go bête in spades and lose 100 points to each opponent.

Tips: Don't count on the widow to provide you the melding help you need. There's just better than a one-in-six chance that one particular card will be there. Even when either of two cards will work, you've only got a one-in-three chance.

In calculating the points you'll lose in play, figure that each opponent may put a high card on your losing tricks.

As defenders, remember the cards you've seen the bidder meld that you can beat. These are cards you should be sure to win. Occasionally the bidder will have even more cards of that suit in his hand, as a "side suit" in addition to trumps.

Variations: Other bidding practices have their own tradition. In one, after two passes the dealer must take with a bid of at least 250. Another format allows the dealer to pass out the hand, or to open it at 290 (but not at 250) or at 320 or higher. A third popular treatment is to require the first hand to start at 300, and be allowed to throw the hand in for the minimum-stake loss.

In *Four-Handed Partnership Pinochle,* partners sit facing each other. Deal 12 cards each, three at a time. Turn up the last card as trumps. If it's a 9, dealer scores 10 points. Otherwise, whoever first has a 9 may replace it with the trump upcard. Players in turn table their melds, which are recorded. Cards are picked up, and the player at dealer's left begins by leading any card. Partners pool their tricks taken, and at the end of play count their points (last trick counts 10). The deal rotates. Game is played to 1000 points.

BÉZIQUE

Bézique, the forerunner of Pinochle, was invented in the early 1800s in Sweden. By the 1850s, it was a hit all across Europe, and it soon arrived in America. It's still widely enjoyed in Britain, where score is kept with individual Bézique "markers."

Number of players: Two.

Object: To score points by melding and by taking tricks containing aces and 10s (called "brisques").

The cards: Two sets of 32 cards, consisting of aces through 7s, are shuffled together into one 64-card deck. Cards rank—from high to low—A-10-K-Q-J-9-8-7.

To play: Deal eight cards to each player (in groups of three, two, and three), and then turn up a card to designate trumps. Place that card face up and slightly sticking out from under the draw pile.

Melds are worth the following amount of points:

Trump marriage (K-Q)	40 points
Non-trump marriage (K-Q in same suit)	20 points
Trump flush (A-10-K-Q-J)	250 points
Bézique (♠Q + ♦J)	40 points
Double Bézique (♠Q + ♦J + ♠Q + ♦J)	500 points
♥A- ♦A-♠A-♣A	100 points
♥K- ♦K-♠K-♣K	80 points
♥Q- ♦Q-♠Q-♣Q	60 points
♥J- ♦J-♠J-♣J	40 points
7 of trumps (each)	10 points

If the trump upcard is a 7, dealer scores 10 points immediately.

Nondealer starts play by leading any card. At this stage of play, and as long as there remain cards to draw, you are not obliged to follow suit, but may play any of your cards.

The highest trump in a trick wins it, or, if there is no trump card, the highest card of the suit led wins it. When two identical cards contend for the same trick (for example, two ♥10s), the first one played wins the trick.

The winner of each trick scores 10 points for each ace or 10 (brisque) it contains, and may also table any one meld. (You may tally the 10 points for a 7 of trumps along with another meld, and if you meld the first 7 of trumps you may also exchange it for the trump upcard.) Tally all points as you score them.

Hearts are trumps. The ♥K and ♥Q form a 40-point marriage. On a later turn, if you are able to add the ♥A-♥10-♥J, you can score another 250 points for the trump flush. Remember that you can make only one meld per turn, and only if you've just won a trick.

Both players take a new card from the stock, with the winner of the previous trick drawing first and then leading to the next trick.

Melded cards stay on the table until the stock is used up, but you may still play them on tricks. A card you meld one time can be used again, but only in a different meld. For example: ♣Q melds with ♣K in a marriage and can also meld later for 60 points with ♥Q-♦Q-♠Q. But it can't meld with a second ♣K—a completely new pair is needed to score the second marriage.

Example of early play: You're dealt ♦Q, ♦7, ♥J, ♥J, ♣A, ♠A, ♠10, *♠Q, with the ♦K upcard. Your first plan is to win a trick in order to exchange your ♦7 for the ♦K, letting you immediately meld a 40-point trump marriage (♦K- ♦Q). You don't want to waste the ♠A, a good melding card, to try to take an early trick. You might try the ♠10, but a less risky choice is one of your ♥Js, which will likely win the trick if your opponent doesn't have a ♥10.*

When only the upcard and one draw card remain, the upcard goes to the trick-loser. Put your remaining melded cards back in your hand, with the winner of the previous trick taking the last draw card and leading to the next trick. In the play of the final eight cards, however, each player must follow suit and also must win a trick whenever possible. Whoever wins the final trick scores an extra 10 points.

| Your hand. | Opponent's hand. |

The last eight tricks of a Bézique hand. Here, diamonds are trumps and it's your lead. If you lead ♥10, followed by ♠J and ♠8, you'll win the brisques for the ♥10s and should also score 10 for last trick with a high trump. See what happens if you start with the ♣K or ♣Q: You'll lose the lead before playing your ♥10, and then your opponent can win both ♥10 brisques and the last trick!

Scoring: The first player to accumulate 1000 points—or any other agreed upon sum—wins.

Tips: The play in Bézique has 32 tricks, most of which occur when your opponent can legally trump any ace or 10 you lead. Therefore, you should save your 10s to win lower cards when your opponent leads. Meanwhile, there's usually a difficult suit for your opponent to win tricks in. Even if you lead low cards of that suit, it may cause discomfort: Players want to hold on to melding cards (aces, kings, queens, the 10 and jack of trumps, and ♠Q and ♦J for a possible 500-point double bézique). Yet each player can hold just eight cards!

If you have a big meld near the end of the game—for example, ♠Q-♠Q-♦J-♦J—you may not have time to meld it in two stages to score an extra 40 points. Your opponent may see through that plan and prevent you from winning a second trick, and the additional 500 points.

Variations: *Rubicon Bézique,* using 128 cards (a double Bézique pack), emphasizes melding. Deal nine cards each. Trumps are fixed by the first marriage melded instead of by turning a trump card up, and new melds include triple bézique (1500 points), quadruple bézique (4500 points), and back door (non-trump A-10-K-Q-J), which counts 150 points.

Every deal is scored independently. The last trick counts 50. No one bothers with brisques, unless the loser needs the brisque points to get over 1000 points and so prevent being rubiconned. The winner of a rubicon game scores a 1000-point bonus instead of 500, gets 320 points for brisques, and gets all of opponent's other points too!

If you're dealt a "carte blanche" (no picture cards), show it and score 50 points, and score 50 more after each draw until you do get a picture card!

You can remake a meld merely by replacing a played melded card!

CANASTA

Canasta—the Spanish word for basket—evolved in Uruguay and spread across Latin America in the 1940s. In 1950, the game swept like wildfire across the United States. Now, nearly a half-century later, Canasta may do so once again.

Number of players: Four, in partnerships seated across the table.

Object: To score points by melding, with the goal of scoring two canastas and then "going out."

The cards: Two regular packs of 52 cards plus their four jokers are used. Jokers and deuces are wild.

Melding: Melds must consist of at least three cards, all of the same rank. All melds are placed face up on the table, and partners build up their melds together to form "canastas"—seven-card bonus melds. All jokers and deuces are wild and can be used in melds as any desired rank except 3s. A canasta must consist of at least four natural cards but may contain any number of wild cards.

The treys: Red 3s are bonus cards worth 100 points each, but they are not used in play. You should lay down a red 3 as soon as you can. If your side scores all four red 3s, the bonus for them doubles to 800 points.

Black 3s are used in play, but are meldable only when "going out." Otherwise, they function as stopper cards (see "Freezing the pack").

To play: Deal 11 cards to each player, one at a time, turning over an upcard that starts a discard pile called the "pack." The remainder of the cards form the stock. Note: If the upcard is a wild card or a red 3, turn another card up on top of it, and see "Freezing the pack."

The player at dealer's left goes first, with play passing in clockwise rotation until the hand is over. At your turn, even on the first round of play, you may "take the pack" with an appropriate hand of cards (see "Taking the pack"), but your usual turn consists of drawing one card and then discarding one card.

Initial melds: The first player to meld for a side must table at least 50 points of meld. All cards have point values for melding.

Joker	50 points
Deuce	20 points
Ace	20 points
King through 8	10 points
7 through 4	5 points
Black 3s	5 points

15 points   **90 points**   **40 points**

To calculate the value of a meld, simply add up the value of the cards it contains. Note that a three-card (or longer) meld must have at least two natural cards.

The initial melding requirement increases along the way as detailed in the table below:

Score at the beginning of new deal	Minimum initial meld
Less than 0	15 points
0–1495	50 points
1500–2995	90 points
3000 or more	120 points

Taking the pack: You are allowed to take the pack—the entire current pile of discards—as long as you can meld the top discard and meet the following conditions. If your side hasn't melded yet, you'll need two natural cards to meld with the upcard, and you must meet the minimum meld required for your side (without using any other cards in the pack). If your side has melded already, then one natural card with one wild card will do, and you may even take the pack if your opponent's discard can go in one of your melds.

You don't have to "take the pack" to make an initial meld, but it gives you more cards to play with. Wait until there are enough cards (around 10 or 12) in the pack to take it, so you will have more cards in your hand. In this case, taking the upcard gives you enough for a 60-point meld: ♥J-♦J-♣J + ♠5-♥5-♣2.

Also, once your side has met its initial meld, you may use the pack to form new melds or add to your melds to form canastas, as you wish. Any cards you don't meld become part of your hand.

Once a meld is on the table, either partner may play off it. When a meld contains seven or more cards, it becomes a canasta. It is squared into a pile and a red card is placed on top if it consists of

Displaying a red card on top of the meld denotes a natural canasta (500 points, no wild cards), while a black card—if available—signals a mixed canasta (300 points, one to three wild cards).

all natural cards (a natural canasta). A black card is placed on top if it contains any wild cards or 3s (a mixed canasta). If any wild cards are later added to a "red" canasta, it becomes a "black" canasta, and its value changes accordingly.

Freezing the pack: Freezing the pack makes it difficult for any player to take the pack. To freeze the pack, discard a wild card sideways across the discards. The next player can't take the pack as long as a wild card remains. To pick up a frozen pack, you'll need a natural pair in your hand. This rule applies to all players, regardless of who froze the pack initially.

A black 3 freezes the pack momentarily, except in the unlikely event that a player with two black 3s can "go out" while taking the pack. That would require using every card taken in the pack. (Note: Wild cards may not meld with black 3s.)

A turn is completed by the player discarding one card face up on the pack.

Going out: You "go out" (sometimes called going "rummy") if you meld all the cards in your hand. However, in order to go out, your side has to have at least one canasta, and in most games you need one card left over to discard. Play ceases at this point, and the score for the hand is tallied.

Before going out, you are allowed to ask your partner "May I go out?" but you must abide by the answer. Should no one go rummy, the hand ends when the stock is gone and the pack can't be taken.

Scoring: Total the value of all melded cards and add bonuses for going rummy (100), natural canastas (500), mixed canastas (300), and red 3s (100 each, but 800 for all four). Subtract the total of cards retained in each player's hand (red 3s count –200 points), and tally each team's score. Game is to 5000 points.

Tip: When taking the pack, don't meld everything in it immediately. It is wise to keep some cards back so that you'll have natural pairs to take a frozen pack.

CASINO

Casino has descended to us directly from Scopa, the old Italian game.

Widely enjoyed as a two- or three-handed game, Casino is also

entertaining for four players—either as partners or "cutthroat" style.

Number of players: Two to four.

Object: To score points by winning cards in play by matching, combining, and building.

The cards: A regular pack of 52 cards is used.

To play: Deal four cards face down to each player and four to the table face up. Keep the remaining cards at hand to deal the following rounds. The player at dealer's left plays the first card of each round, with play continuing in clockwise order. When all players have played their four cards, the same dealer deals four more cards to each player. Cards are dealt to the table only in the first round, however.

At your turn, you might simply place a card on the table (see "Trailing"). However, there are several ways to take cards—or to try to take them: by matching, by combining, by building, and by taking another player's build.

A Casino hand (top) and table layout (bottom).

You can combine the card you play with the cards on the table in many possible ways. Suits do not matter.

Matching: If your card matches the rank of a card on the table, you can take the pair immediately, placing them in your own stack face down in front of you. In the illustrated hand, you can take the ♥Q with the ♣Q, or you can take the ♠7 with the ♦7. Face cards match in pairs only—when two kings are on the table and you hold one king in your hand, you capture only one of the kings. However, if three kings are dealt to the table, whoever has the fourth king takes them all. Plain cards can match in greater numbers.

Combining: If your card equals the combined sum of two or more cards on the table, you can take the cards immediately. In the deal shown, you may combine the ♣6 and ♣2 and take them away with the ♦8.

Building: If at least one card on the table plus the card you play totals another card in your hand, announce this build number and pile the build-cards together. In the example shown, play the ♠A onto the ♠7, and say "Building 8s." You may also put the ♣6 and ♣2 into this build, making it a "multiple build." On your next turn—if no one's taken your build—you can pick it up with your ♦8. (And, if you have no other build or capture, you must.) At your turn, you can take an opponent's build when you have the right card, and, of course, an opponent can take yours as well.

Occasionally, with the right holding, you can increase an opponent's build. With a deuce and a 10, play the deuce on top of a simple 8-build and announce "Building 10s." Multiple builds, by the way, can't be built up to a higher number.

Trailing: If you have nothing else to do on your turn, you must trail a card—place it on the table without building it onto another card. You cannot do this if you have made a build that's still on the table.

When dealing the last round, call "Last" to alert the other players. Whoever takes the final cards on the last round also wins any untaken cards remaining at the end.

Scoring: Players count their cards and note the cards with extra value. Each deal has 11 points.

♦10 (Big Casino)	2 points
♠2 (Little Casino)	1 point
Each ace	1 point
"Spades" (Player who takes the most spades)	1 point
"Cards" (Player who takes the most cards)	3 points

When there's a tie for "cards" in a two-player game, neither scores for it. In a three-handed game, those tied score 2 points each; in larger games, those tied score 1 point each.

Play to 21 points, or to any other agreed upon number.

Tips: The more players in a game, the riskier it is to build. In a four-handed game, someone is likely to take a build made early in the round, so try to delay your build, if possible.

The fewer players in a game, the more you can control the action. It will help to know which key cards remain—10s, aces, and other high building cards. A skilled player in a two-handed game knows which cards have been played and which cards are left for the final round.

Variations: In *Scoops,* 1 point is scored for a "scoop"—a play that clears the table. Signify scoops by facing one card up for each.

Continuous Casino: Deal as in regular Casino, but leave the stock of undealt cards in everybody's reach. In this game, take a new card after each play. No further rounds of cards are dealt. (This method can accommodate five players.)

Partnership Casino: Teammates sit across from each other, keeping winnings together and trying, within the rules, to help each other.

CONCENTRATION

The most appropriately named game of all time! "Concentration" is what you'll need to win this game. Since children sometimes are better at this game than adults are, it can be an enjoyable pastime for the entire family.

Number of players: Two or more.

Object: To gather in the most cards by matching them in pairs.

The cards: A regular pack of 52 cards is used.

To play: You'll need a large surface area. Deal the whole deck out, card by card, face down. It doesn't matter if the cards are in neat rows or in a haphazard arrangement.

These two cards don't match, but remember where they are for later play!

By tradition, the youngest player goes first. Each turn consists of turning up one card and then another, taking care to keep them in place. When the two cards match in rank, put them in your winnings pile and continue your turn, revealing two new cards.

However, when the cards you turn over are of different rank, your turn ends. Return them to their places, face down. Try to concentrate on remembering where each card lies, as you may still pair one or the other later.

Scoring: When the cards have all been matched, record the number of cards you've taken. Whoever has the most cards after three games wins.

Tip: Concentration rewards visual recall, and some people are just better at this than others. This tip can help you keep pace: Say you've just seen another player turn the ♥5 and you suspect you remember the location of a 5 seen earlier. When your turn comes, go first for the earlier 5, not for the ♥5. When you're right, all you have to do is grab the ♥5 (but don't forget where *it* is). This way, if the first card you turn over is not a 5, you've still got a chance to find a match for it!

Variations: With a very young crowd of players, you may want to omit some cards for a smaller layout. For example, you may wish to leave out all aces, 3s, 5s, 7s, and 9s.

For a more advanced crowd, play *Moving Concentration*: You may return pairs that don't match to new spots in the layout!

COON CAN

A game that appears to have originated down South, "Coon Can" comes from the Spanish ¿con quién? (meaning "with what?"). Also known as Conquian, it is one of the few rummy games that has lasted over a century. Perhaps its colorful lingo contributes to its long-term appeal.

Number of players: Two.

Object: To "go coon can," that is to meld all your cards, plus an extra card you pick from the draw or discard pile. As in most rummy games, melds must be at least three cards long.

The cards: A 40-card pack (akin to a Spanish pack), with all 10s, 9s, and 8s removed, is used. This leaves the jack and 7 in sequence. Aces are low.

Rank order in Coon Can.

Melding: Melds in Coon Can must have at least three cards and are left on the table.

      Short spreads.   *Long spreads.*

To play: Deal ten cards each and leave the rest face down as a draw pile. Nondealer begins by plucking (turning up) and showing the top card from stock. You cannot add a plucked card to your hand, so if this card is not used in a meld, it must be discarded. Each player in turn must either take the top discard and meld it, or turn up the top card from stock and add it to a spread or discard it.

During one turn, you may hit your own spreads with any number of cards, but when you hit your opponent's spread, that's consid-

Coon Can's terminology:

Hit (noun). A card laid off on a meld.

Hit (verb). To lay a card off on a meld.

Hole. A hand you can't go coon can with.

Long spread. Suit sequence meld.

Pluck. To pick a card from stock.

Short spread. Meld of the same rank.

Sleep it. To purposely overlook a play.

Switch. To move a card from one meld to another.

ered your discard. Actually, when your spread is hit by your opponent, you have 11 cards. You must discard from your hand instead of plucking a new card!

You may shift your own melds around to create new melds as long as you leave only valid melds behind.

In Coon Can, you can move cards from one meld to another (switch) as long as you leave only legal spreads.

If you go coon can (have 11 cards in spreads), the game ends and you win the agreed stake. Occasionally, no one goes coon can—a "tab game"—and the stake for it is added to the next game.

Tips: A good amount of skill is involved in hitting your opponent with the intent of forcing a discard from his hand. This discard may be a card you can use, or it may spoil your adversary's plans. Also, you may be able to force your opponent into a "hole"—a hand that can't go coon can. For instance, a hand that's a ten-card-long spread (a spread of an entire suit, for example) can't go coon can, since an eleventh card is required.

Forcing: Opponent shows these two spreads. When you "hit" with ♠Q, it forces the discard of one of the two concealed cards.

"Sleeping it": Discarding a card that could match one's own spread may often be a good strategy, but it can be stopped. When you see your opponent "sleeping it," you may force your opponent to hit with it instead, forcing a further discard.

Variations: People who are uncomfortable with placing a 7 and jack in sequence may instead use a 40-card pack, aces through 10s, removing all face cards.

Some games permit players to pluck a card just "on speculation," rather than requiring it to be immediately melded or added to a spread.

CRAZY EIGHTS

Eights are wild and so is the action in this fast-paced game the whole family can play. An easy-to-learn game that calls for a lot of luck, Crazy Eights is a very good game to play with kids.

Number of players: Two to six. Even more can play, but the more players, the longer each person has to wait between turns.

Object: To be the first player to get rid of all your cards.

The cards: A regular pack of 52 cards is used, but with four or more players you might want to use two packs!

To play: Deal seven cards to each player, turn one card up to start a discard pile, and leave the remainder of the cards next to the pile as a draw stack. The player at dealer's left begins by covering the upcard with a matching card—one that's either the same suit or same rank. For example, if the starter is ♦7, any diamond or any 7 can be played. Whenever you can't match, draw cards from stock until you find a match.

All 8s are wild and can be played at any time. Call the 8 any suit; the next player must match it. (Don't specify a rank.)

It's your turn to match the ♥4. Choose ♣4, ♥Q, or ♥9. Save the wild card (♦8) for when you really need it!

Play rotates to the left, as each player matches the top card, and continues until one player has no cards left. If you run out of draw cards along the way, simply turn over the discard pile, shuffle well, and use it for a new face-down draw pile.

Scoring: Whoever goes out scores the point total of cards left in everyone else's hands. Each 8 counts 50, face cards count 10, and all others count their pip value (ace = 1). The game usually ends after an agreed time limit or number of deals.

Tips: When you have many cards of one suit, others may find that suit hard to match. Remember, in a game with several players, your play affects the next player most.

Don't get caught holding wild cards at the end of play, since they count a whopping 50 points each!

Variations: In *No-Shuffle Crazy Eights,* once the stock is gone, pass when you have no play. Sometimes a "blocked" game results, where no one can match the top discard and no one has an 8. When this occurs, players count their points, and whoever has the lowest total wins the difference in hand-count from each other player.

Double Crazy Eights: Turn the upcard sideways so that two piles can fit on it. As play goes on, you may choose which pile to play on. You may still play an 8 anytime, but you must match it next by its own suit.

CRIBBAGE

This quietly appealing game, which has been played for more than 350 years, is in a class by itself. It may take you a few moments to learn, but once you pick it up you'll begin to admire its many chances for thought and strategy. Since scoring occurs at nearly every moment, a cribbage board is very useful for scoring, or "pegging."

Number of players: Two to four. The two-handed game will be described first.

Object: To score points for certain card combinations and be the first to peg 121 points (or 61, as agreed).

The cards: A regular pack of 52 cards is used. Each card has a point value equal to its rank. Aces are low and count 1. Face cards count 10.

To play: Deal six cards to each player. Both players then select two cards to discard for a face-down, four-card "crib" belonging to the dealer. The goal in discarding is to retain a hand of four cards that will form scoring combinations.

Nondealer selects ♥8, ♦K to discard for the crib.

Dealer selects ♠5, ♠J to discard for the crib.

The dealer lays the crib aside without looking at it, and it is not used until after the play.

Scoring combinations:

Fifteen: any combination of cards totaling exactly 15	2 points
Pair: two cards of the same rank	2 points
Triplet: three cards of the same rank	6 points
Quartet: four cards of the same rank	12 points
Sequence: three or more cards in a row, any suit	1 point per card
Flush: any four cards of the same suit	1 point per card
His Nobs: jack of the starter's suit, in hand	1 point

Note that flushes and His Nobs don't score during play.

Next, nondealer cuts the pack and dealer turns up the top card (the "start" or "starter"). If the start is a jack, dealer scores 2 points for "His Nobs." The starter card is not used in play. The remaining cards form the stock, which is not used in this hand.

Nondealer now plays one card face up, calling out its value. Dealer does the same, calling the total of the two cards played. Continue in this way as long as the count doesn't exceed 31. Keep cards in two separate piles—one for dealer's cards, one for nondealer's cards. When you can't play without exceeding 31, say "Go," which instructs your opponent to continue play without going past 31, as opponent pegs 1 for your "go." If opponent is able to reach 31 exactly after your "go," he pegs 2 instead of 1 (1 for 31, 1 for "go"). When both players are unable to play, a new count is begun by the player who didn't make the last play. Playing the last card of all counts 1 point.

Pegging for melds made in play: Cards must be played consecutively within one 31-count to score. In addition to the scoring for "go," 31, and the last card, combinations made during play also score points. If your play makes the count 15, score 2. If you match the rank of the card played by opponent, score 2 for the pair. Three cards of the same rank are worth 6 points, and the fourth one scores 12. Sequences also count, and the cards don't have to be in exact order. Example: 3-6-4-5 scores 4 points for the last player, and if the next player follows with a deuce, that sequence is worth 5 points. A flush (series of cards of the same suit) does not score in play; it scores only when scoring the hand.

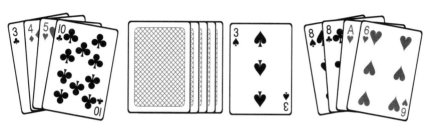

Nondealer starts by saying "Three." Dealer plays the ♠8 and says "11." Nondealer plays ♦4 and says "15 for 2" while pegging 2. This is followed by "23," "28," "29," and "go." Dealer also cannot play under 31 but pegs 1 for nondealer's "go." Nondealer begins the new count by playing the ♣10 and calling "Ten." "Sixteen and last," says dealer, pegging 1.

Scoring the hands: After you've played out the cards, nondealer's hand is counted and pegged (see "Scoring combinations"), followed by dealer's hand, and then dealer's crib. This order is important because if at any point either player reaches 121 (or 61), the game is immediately ended. The start card is scored as a fifth card in each hand.

The board has 30 holes in each of the long rows, marked off in groups of five. Each player gets two pegs. In the beginning, the four pegs sit at the start end of the board. The pegs move up the outside and down the inside back to the start, for a total of 61 points. The usual game is two trips, or 121 points. The two pegs are used alternately, the back peg leap-frogging over the front peg.

In the illustrated hand (above), nondealer pegs 12: two sequences (3-4-5, 3-4-5), one pair (3s), and two 15s (5-10, 3-3-4-5). Dealer pegs 6: two 15s (8-6-A, 8-6-A) and a pair (8s). By custom, non-dealer now separates the start card, gathers in the rest, and dealer pegs the crib. In this case, (see page 27) it's worth 5: two 15s (5-J, 5-K) and His Nobs (♠J).

At the end of each hand, all the cards (from dealer's hand, non-dealer's hand, crib, and stock) are gathered and shuffled together to form a fresh pack of 52 for the next hand. Nondealer from last hand becomes dealer for new hand.

Pegging out: As soon as you peg to 121 (or to 61, as agreed), the game ends, no matter when this occurs. If the loser fails to score at least 61 points in a game of 121, he is "skunked," or "lurched," and the winner scores for a double game.

Tips: In play, start with a card under 5 so that the next player can't peg a quick 2 points for 15. Hold back your low cards to help score for "go" or 31. Also, keep an eye open for surprise sequences. For instance, if the first cards are a 6 and a 2, and a 3, 4, and 5 are the next cards (in any order), peg 5 points!

Keep in mind who gets the crib when you contribute to it. Pairs or 5s put in your own crib can be better than holding them, but give your opponent high and low cards—say a queen and a 2. Also, since you discard for the crib right away, consider how the cards you keep might fit with various start cards.

Near the end of the game, desperate strategies may be called for. For example, if you are dealer and both you and your opponent need a few points to win, you'll need to peg out in play, since your opponent's hand scores ahead of yours. Therefore, keep cards that can score points in play—forget about making a high-scoring hand.

Variations: If your opponent fails to peg for a score, call "Muggins" and peg the points yourself. Friendly games often omit this rule.

Cribbage for Three: Each player competes independently. If you're using a cribbage board, two players will have to peg up and down a single line of pegging-holes.

Deal five cards to each player, and one card to the crib. Each player then chooses one card to add to the crib. For the start card, dealer offers either adversary the cut. Player at dealer's left then starts play, which proceeds clockwise. "Go" still scores 1 point; and if two players in succession say "go" it still pegs 1. (With three players, you may receive a point for "go" and later in the same count say "go" yourself.)

Cribbage for Four: Although this can be played "cutthroat" style—each player on his or her own—more commonly it's a partnership game, played with the partners facing each other.

Deal five cards to each player. Each player then donates one card to the crib. Only one player pegs for each side, with the cribbage board placed between these two players. Partners may, however, point out counts or melds to each other.

DEMON

This is a solitaire game played by many people at once, with everybody building on common piles. Action and noise can reach high levels, so you may need to keep a whistle handy!

Number of players: Two to eight.

Object: To play out more cards than any other player.

The cards: A regular pack of 52 cards is used per player. Each pack should have a different back design.

To play: Each player deals a layout for the solitaire widely known as "Klondike" (called "Canfield" in England). Refer to the diagram below for the proper layout.

To achieve this layout, first deal a row of seven cards with the left-most one face up and the rest face down. On top of the face-down cards, deal another row, with the leftmost of these face up. Keep doing this until you have seven piles, ranging from one card on the left to seven cards on the right, with the top cards face up. The remainder of the cards form the stock.

Wait for all players to complete their layouts. At a signal, turn over three cards from stock to start your "waste heaps," and begin making plays. Once the game is underway, play at your own pace.

There are several moves available to you. You should release your aces into the center of the table as soon as possible, where any player can build them up in sequence by suit, ending with the king. These piles are called "foundation piles."

You can build downward sequences on the cards in your layout, in alternating suit color only. For example, the ♥10 can be moved upon the ♣J, but not on the ♦J. Play cards onto the center foundation piles as available. Note that everyone can play onto each foundation pile, but each player can only play onto his own layout.

When you move a card from its pile, turn up the card beneath. Occasionally a pile empties, opening up a vacancy. You can fill this only with a king or with a sequence headed by a king.

The topmost card of your waste heap is always available for play, as is any single card on a pile, and also the topmost (lowest) card of a sequence.

In the illustrated hand, move the ♦8 onto the ♠9, move both to the ♥10, and move these to the ♣J. All of these end up on the ♥Q! What a start! You're left with one empty pile and three new cards to turn up.

When you've gone through the stock, three cards at a time, turn your waste heap over to make a new stock. You can continue to do this as often as you like. At some point you may run out of plays, but as other players develop their layouts, your cards may become eligible to play in the center, and you may find several more plays.

The game ends when one player's cards have all been played into the middle. That player shouts "Demon," and all further play ceases. The cards on foundation piles are then sorted out to return to each player. (The game is also considered ended when no player can find a play.)

Scoring: A player going out scores 52 points plus a 10-point bonus, and everyone else gets 1 point per card in the foundation piles. One player keeps a tally for everyone, and at the end of an agreed upon number of deals the winner is the one with the highest total score.

Note: Not infrequently, two players will attempt to play the same card on the same foundation pile. Whoever's card is at the bottom is deemed to have gotten there first.

Tips: Fast action is a key to winning, so set yourself up to make quick consecutive plays to the foundation piles.

Keep the center orderly by turning over the foundation piles that have been completely built up to king.

To keep the game alive, you may point out plays to another player.

Variation: Play solitaires other than Klondike that offer common scoring piles for all players.

EUCHRE

❖

Euchre is thought to have descended directly from Triomphe, an

immensely popular sixteenth-century game. A hundred years ago in

America, Euchre had plenty of devotees, and was considered our

national game!

❖

Number of players: Four, with partners seated facing each other. Euchre may also be played by two or three players.

Object: To score points by winning at least three of five tricks.

The cards: A 32-card pack, aces through 7s for each suit, is used. All 2s through 6s are discarded before play. Cards rank as follows: A-K-Q-J-10-9-8-7, except in trumps, where the jack—called the "right bower"—is high, and the other jack of the same color—the "left bower"—is the second highest trump.

Rank of cards in trumps, with clubs trump.

To play: Deal five cards to each player, in bunches of two and three, or three and two, and turn up the next card to propose a trump suit. If that suit becomes the trump suit, the upcard replaces another in dealer's hand. By custom, it stays on the table, while the card it replaces is put beneath the remaining undealt cards.

Determining the trump suit: Starting at dealer's left, each player has a chance to accept or pass the suit turned as trumps. To accept, an opponent of the dealer says "I order it up," dealer's partner says "I assist," and dealer accepts by discarding. Any player may pass.

On balance, to "accept" you should judge your side at least a two-to-one favorite, since you win only 1 point when you succeed (unless you score a march), but lose 2 points when you fail (see "Scoring").

If all four players pass, dealer places the upcard under the pack of undealt cards, and another round follows, to find a trump suit. Starting with the player at dealer's left, each may pass until one player names a trump suit other than the suit first turned up. If all players again pass, throw the cards in and shuffle for a new deal.

When accepting or naming a trump suit, you may also declare at that time to "play alone." Your partner's hand is put aside, and you play against both opponents.

The player at dealer's left usually leads to the first trick, but when you play a lone hand, the defender at your left leads first.

On each trick, follow to the suit of the card led if possible. Otherwise, play any card. Each trick is won by the highest card of the suit led, except a trick containing at least one trump, which is won by the highest trump played. Note that the ♥J is not considered a heart when diamonds are trumps!

Scoring:

Declaring side wins three or four tricks	1 point
Declaring side wins five tricks (a "march")	2 points
If "lone hand"	4 points
Declaring side "euchred" (wins fewer than three tricks), opponents score	2 points

Game is played to a predetermined amount of points, usually 5, 7, or 10.

Tips: The trump suit has nine cards, but there are only seven cards in the other suit of the same color. The two remaining suits have eight cards each. Since each deal leaves out about a third of the deck, on average only five or six cards of each suit are in play. If you have three cards in the trump suit and your partner can take a trick, you are likely to win the majority of tricks.

When you have three practically certain winning cards in your hand and chances of winning the other cards, it may be wise to play alone. Your non-trump cards, even if not clear winners, may take tricks anyway: Your opponents have only ten cards between them, and may fail to hold on to the right cards!

Don't forget that if the upcard is accepted as trumps, it becomes part of the dealer's hand. This may influence your decision to accept that suit as trumps for your side.

The "game" score may also influence your decision to pass, accept, or play alone. If you have a large lead, it may be a good risk to venture a questionable acceptance of the trump suit if you fear an opponent may score a march (4 points) in a different suit. Even if you're euchred, opponent scores only 2 points.

Variations: *Two-Handed Euchre* is generally played with a 24-card pack, omitting 7s and 8s as well. Score for "march" is 2 points, and the option to declare a lone hand does not exist.

Three-Handed Euchre: The player who makes trumps plays against the other two, who temporarily unite as partners. The scoring is as follows:

Maker of trump suit wins three or four tricks	1 point
Maker of trump suit wins five tricks (a "march")	3 points
Maker of trump suit is euchred, each opponent wins	2 points

Railroad Euchre: A joker is added as the highest trump, regardless of suit.

FAN TAN

Don't confuse Fan Tan—also known as Card Dominoes, Sevens, and Parliament—with "Chinese Fan Tan," an unrelated gambling game.

Number of players: Three to eight, but the game is best when four play.

Object: To be the first to play off all your cards.

The cards: A regular pack of 52 cards is used. Aces are low.

To play: Give each player an equal supply of chips; you'll need a bowl or a dish to collect them in. Deal one card at a time to each player, until the whole pack is dealt. It doesn't matter if some players have one card fewer than the others.

Beginning with the player at dealer's left, each player must play a 7, or else add on to cards in suit-sequences ascending or descending from the 7s.

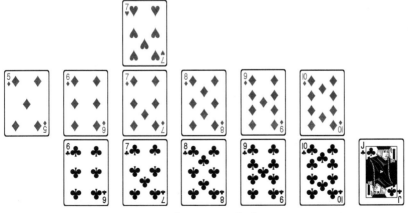

A Fan Tan game in progress after several plays.

Once the ♦7 has been played, for example, the ♦8 and ♦6 can be played. If the ♦8 is played, you can play the ♦9, and so on. Sequences ascend to the king and descend to the ace. Once an end card is reached, fold up the row of cards and turn them over.

Whenever you have no card to play, pass and toss one chip into the "kitty." Whoever is out of cards first collects the chips in the kitty, plus one chip per card left in each player's hand.

Tips: Try to encourage play in suits where you have aces or kings. Your goal is to be able to hold back "stoppers": the 5s, 6s, 8s, and 9s that block everyone else's cards but not your own. If your timing is right, the suits you need help in will open up before your stoppers are gone.

GO FISH

For many of us, Go Fish was our first card game, and for

some of us, it may still be the one we play best!

Number of players: Two to six.

Object: To win the most sets of four cards ("books") by asking other players for them.

The cards: A regular pack of 52 cards is used, but you might "shorten" the pack for a quicker game by removing all cards of a few different ranks.

To play: When two people play, deal seven cards each; otherwise, deal five cards each. Leave the undealt cards face down as a draw pile. Starting with the player at dealer's left, each player asks another for cards of a specific rank. For example: "Kevin, do you have any 6s?" In order to ask, you yourself must already have at least one 6. Kevin has to give you all the 6s he holds, but the other players do not.

Whenever your request for a card is filled, it remains your turn. Continue with your turn, asking any player for cards of a specific rank. When the player you ask can't oblige, you'll be told to "Go Fish." Pick up the top card of the draw pile. If it's the rank you called for, show the card at once, and your turn goes on. Otherwise, your turn ends.

If this is your hand, you can ask for 6s, 3s, 8s, Ks, 9s, or aces.

Play proceeds to the left in this fashion. Whenever you have collected all four cards of one rank (a "book"), show the other players, then place the book next to you in a compact pile.

Scoring: When all the cards have been drawn and all the books collected, whoever has the most books wins.

Tip: Pay attention to who seeks which cards, for you will certainly draw a card someone was looking for earlier. You'll capture those cards at your next turn if you can remember whom to ask!

Variations: Call for cards from all players at once: The game moves faster when everyone must give up the wanted cards. This also makes it a better move to ask for a card when your book lacks just one, since whoever might have drawn the fourth one must give it to you.

An interesting scoring variant is to give each book a value equal to its rank. Aces can count 11, picture cards 10, and all others their pip value.

HEARTS

In any of its numerous versions, Hearts is not difficult to play, but it's

certainly not easy to master. An observant and calculating player will

be a consistent winner. Actually, Hearts is a game for the loser in us,

for if you hold a lot of low cards, you'll win!

Number of players: Four is best, but three or six may also play. The four-player version is explained first.

Object: To win as few of the penalty cards as possible (all the hearts as well as the ♠Q), or else—if the hand is strong enough—to win them all.

Point-scoring cards in Hearts. Try not to take these cards, or else try to take them all!

The cards: A regular pack of 52 cards is used. Aces are high.

To play: Deal cards one at a time, until each player has 13.

The pass: A most interesting feature of Hearts is the pass, where each player sends three cards to another player. A popular method is to pass the cards to the left on the first deal, to the right on the second deal, and across on the third deal, with no pass at all on the fourth deal. The cycle then repeats. Players may not look at the cards passed to them until they have completed their own pass.

Whoever holds the ♣2 now leads it. Follow suit if possible but if you can't, play any card other than a heart or the ♠Q. Whoever plays the highest card of the suit led wins the trick and leads to the next. For example, whoever plays the highest club on the first trick takes the cards played to that trick, and leads to the next.

Breaking hearts: You can't lead a heart until hearts have been "broken"—that is, until someone has discarded a heart already. However, if it's your lead and all you have are hearts, you must lead one.

Scoring: After all the tricks have been played out, count up the penalty cards you've taken. Count 1 for each heart, and 13 for the ♠Q. For instance, if your tricks include the ♠Q and the ♥6, ♥7, ♥9, ♥10, and ♥K, you would receive 18 points. The other three players would score the remaining 8 points. Keep a running tally. The game ends when someone reaches 100 points or any agreed upon sum. Whoever has the lowest score at the end is the winner.

Shooting the moon: If the tricks you win contain all the hearts and the ♠Q, this is called "shooting the moon." Subtract 26 points from your score if you accomplish this. (If you choose, you may add 26 points to everyone else's score. This would end the game more quickly.)

Tips: You generally want to avoid taking tricks; however, on most hands, you'll take a few. Your main concern is always to avoid the trick that includes the ♠Q. This affects the pass especially. If you are dealt the ♠Q, you may be safer keeping it if you have at least five spades. Otherwise it may be a danger in your hand and you should pass it, for the other players will lead spades. The ♠A and ♠K are risky to keep when you are "short" in spades, since they may be forced to capture the dreaded ♠Q. Spades lower than the ♠Q are usually very safe to keep, since none can capture the ♠Q!

Sometimes it's best to pass all your cards in a "short" suit with no low cards, since you'd be forced to win tricks in that suit otherwise. On some hands it may be wise to pass cards in a variety of suits, to increase the likelihood of everyone following suit.

Your hand before a right-hand pass. You should pass the ♠Q, ♦9, and ♥6. With the ♠Q on your right, the ♠A is not a dangerous card! If you were passing left, you'd pass the ♠A instead of the ♥6.

If you are thinking of shooting the moon, pass away all hearts that might be losers, since suspicious players will not let you win any hearts of mid-rank if they suspect you're shooting.

Variations: There's practically an infinite number of ways that Hearts can be played, so make sure everyone is playing by the same rules. One popular rule is that the ♠Q must be discarded at its first available opportunity. This avoids accusations of a player holding it to "dump" on a specific opponent. Another widespread rule is to count either the ♦J or ♦10 as –10 points in favor of whoever wins it.

In some games, the pass is always to the left, while some prefer no pass at all; in others, the ♣2 isn't required to be led—instead, the player at dealer's left may lead any card at all.

For three players, discard the ♦2, leaving 51 cards, and deal 17 cards to each player. Pass four cards, not three. With more or fewer than four players, you can pass left and right, but not across.

I DOUBT IT

————◆◆————

I Doubt It is a hilarious game that is fun for children as well as adults.

If you're the sneaky sort and have a suspicious mind,

then this game is for you!

————◆◆————

Number of players: Two or more, but it's a greater challenge with at least three players.

Object: To be the first player to get rid of all your cards.

The cards: A regular pack of 52 cards is used for two to five players. Two packs of 52 cards are used for six or more players.

To play: Deal all the cards out, as evenly as possible. To save time, deal in twos or threes.

In turn, players discard one or more cards, announcing them by rank. Start with aces.

The player at dealer's left begins by saying, for example, "Two aces," placing two cards face down in the center of the table to begin a discard stack.

The following player announces "Deuces"—or perhaps "One deuce"—and puts a single card face down on the stack. The next player announces "3s" and so on, each player stating a rank just above the previous one. After you reach kings, start again at aces.

At your turn you must discard, but the cards you discard don't have to be the rank called for. You might announce "Three queens" and put two jacks and a 6, or any three cards. Be convincing. Anyone can challenge you by being first to shout "I doubt it!"

Lay successive discard packets crosswise, to avoid disputes. Here, a player has announced four 7s but has been caught playing two 6s, a 3, and an 8!

The challenge: If challenged, turn over your discards. If they're not what you claimed, pick up the entire discard pack. But if your cards are as announced, your challenger picks up the stack!

Note that when you use a single pack, you can discard up to four cards. With a double deck, the discard can go as high as eight cards.

Tips: Often you'll need to make a phony discard. This may be easier to do when the discard stack is low. You may get away with a one-card lie.

As the pile grows, so do the risks of discarding and challenging. Also, you're sure to be challenged on your final discard. So, plan ahead to have at least one card of the rank you'll need.

It can be helpful to expand your hand by losing an occasional challenge.

Variation: In some games, there may be too many challenges, and you may want to bring order to them. One way to do this is to permit only the next player to say "I doubt it."

KALUKI

Spell it Kalooki, Caloochi, Kalogghi, or whatever, but this double-deck rummy game has been a longtime club favorite in America and Great Britain.

Number of players: Two to six.

Object: To be the first player to get rid of all the cards in your hand by creating melds.

The cards: Two regular packs of 52 cards plus their four jokers are used. Aces are high or low, but not both.

To play: With two to four players, deal 15 cards each. With five players, deal 13 to each, and with six, deal 11 each. Then turn one card up to start the discard pile. The remaining cards form the stock. A player cannot take the upcard until he has made an initial meld or can use the upcard immediately in a meld. Your first meld must total at least 51 points, which can include cards you lay off on other players' melds as long as you table at least one meld of your own.

Value of cards in melding:

Ace	15 points
Face card	10 points
Plain card	pip value
Joker	value of the card it stands for

Melds are three or more cards of the same rank (no repeated suits), or three or more cards of the same suit in sequence. Aces can be high or low, but not both. For example, ◆Q-◆K-◆A and ◆A-◆2-◆3 are valid melds, but ◆K-◆A-◆2 is not.

Before your initial meld, when it is your turn, either take the upcard if you can meld it, or else take the top card from stock, meld if able, and discard. After your initial meld, you are entitled to pick the card showing and discard from your hand without melding. Whenever you meld, you may also lay off cards on your own and other players' melds.

Pick up the ♦2 for a sequence (9 points), and use the joker as an ace, counting 15 (45 points). Since 9 + 45 = 54 points, you are able to meld. This doesn't even take into account any layoffs you may be able to make.

Your hand.

Tabled meld.

At your turn of play, you may swap a card for a joker that's melded as that card. In this meld, if you have the ♦9, exchange it for the joker, which you can use later however you choose.

Scoring: Each losing player pays the winner 1 point per card left in hand, and 2 points per joker left in hand. A player who goes out on a single play goes "Kaluki" and collects double from every player.

Tips: Usually it doesn't take many rounds for someone to go out, so there's no real advantage to delaying your initial meld.

Jokers are valuable. While they can be melded as a group for 15 points each, they are put to much better use individually.

Variations: In scoring, an alternate practice is to penalize players for the face value of the cards in their hand, with jokers counting 25 points each.

One version of Kaluki counts aces as 11, not 15, so agree among players about this beforehand.

MICHIGAN

———◆◆◆———

The many names of this game—Chicago, Saratoga, Newmarket, Stops,
Boodle, and others—show its far-reaching appeal. Though played with
cards and chips, it involves no betting.

———◆◆◆———

Number of players: Two or more.

Object: To win chips by being the first player out of cards, and also
by playing "money" or "boodle" cards.

The cards: A regular pack of 52 cards is used, plus an extra ♥A,
♣K, ♠Q, and ♦J (the "boodle" cards). Aces are high.

To play: Distribute an equal number of chips to each player. Place
the four boodle cards face up in the center of the table, where they
remain throughout play. Each player puts one chip on each boodle
card.

The layout of boodle cards.

Deal all the cards out, one at a time,
dealing one hand more than players.
For example, if there are four players,
deal five hands. The extra hand,
called the "widow," is dealt to dealer's
left. It's all right if some players have
one more card than others.

As dealer, look at your cards and
decide if you wish to exchange them
for the widow (without seeing it first).
If you prefer, keep your original hand
and auction the widow, still unseen, to
the other players. The auction begins

at one chip. Collect the chips bid for it, and keep them in your own hand. The high bidder wins the widow hand and must play it, but this player retains an advantage in knowing which cards will be out of play.

The player at dealer's left leads the lowest card held of any suit. Whoever has the next card in sequence in that suit plays it, and so on, until no one can play. For example, the ♥4 is led, the same player also plays the ♥5, and then other players follow with the ♥6, ♥7, and ♥8. No one has the ♥9, a "stopper," so whoever played the ♥8 now continues play, leading the lowest card of a different suit.

When an ace is played, the sequence ends. As always, begin a new sequence with your lowest card in another suit. Whenever you play a boodle card, collect the chips on it. If you play your last card, the deal ends and you win, collecting the chips in the kitty and also one chip from each player for every card you catch them with. The deal also ends when no one can play.

This hand has no boodle cards, no aces, and no other high cards to finish off the run of a suit. If this is your hand as dealer, swap it for the widow. If you're not the dealer, you should bid for the widow and get rid of this hand.

Leave all uncollected chips on the boodle cards. The deal passes to the left, and all players put another chip on each boodle card. Since the dealer has an advantage, the game ends after an agreed number of complete dealing rounds. Whoever has the most chips is the winner.

erwise. Each trick is taken by the highest card in it of the suit led, or by the highest trump if it contains any trump. The winner of each trick leads to the following trick.

In a five-handed game, you hold this hand. Bid "One." You'll take the ace of trumps—it's a sure winner. If you're careful, you won't take another trick! Spades probably won't be led three times, and even so, the ♠10 shouldn't be a problem. The ♥5 is not likely to win, and the key will be to save the ♦3, a low trump, for a trick containing higher trumps. An ideal scenario would be for a club to be led, so you could trump it with the ♦A and then lead the ♦3.

Scoring: After all the tricks have been taken, the scorekeeper tallies how everyone fared. If you made your bid exactly, score 1 point per trick plus a 10-point bonus. (With the example hand, you'd score 11.) If you failed, however, subtract 10 points for each trick you're off, whether it's more or less than your bid. The player with the most points after the last deal wins. It's not unusual to end up with a negative score, by the way.

Tips: Bidding in the first few rounds can be tricky, since so few cards from the pack are in play, and some bids are forced. In the early deals, you'll be surprised to see your low cards win tricks, while your aces get trumped. In most deals, you can count on low cards to be losers more reliably than counting on high cards to be winners (unless they're high trumps).

When the bid-total is above the number of tricks in the deal, other players will be quite willing to capture your questionable middle-range cards or trump a trick that you have the high card on. However, when the bid-total is under the trick-total, players will be happy to let you win an extra trick or two.

Variations: Some players prefer to write down bids secretly. In this case, it's okay for the bid-total and the trick-total to turn out equal. Those bids can be revealed either before the first lead or after the last trick.

In many games, once the highest possible number of cards have been dealt, the game continues with the number of cards per hand decreasing by one each hand, until a final one-card deal.

OLD MAID

Many of us think Old Maid requires a special pack of cards, but actually its ancestral form some 150 years ago likely used a regular pack minus one card.

Number of players: Three or more is best, though two can play.

Object: Not to be left holding the "Old Maid."

The cards: A pack of 51 cards is used, made by removing one queen from a regular pack.

To play: Deal all the cards out one at a time. Before play starts, each player shows and retires any pairs of like rank. After that, the player at dealer's left takes one card, unseen, from the player at his left. If this makes a pair, it is also tabled, and the player continues.

When the card taken does not make a pair, play passes on to the next player, who in turn takes a card from the next player. In this way all cards eventually pair up except one queen, and the player holding it is declared "Old Maid."

Draw cards from your neighbor's hand, seeing the card backs only.

Tip: After one pair of queens has been tabled, only body language can tell you who might have the remaining lone queen. Even so, it's hard to know which card that queen might be. Is the player in the diagram encouraging you to take the card sticking out? Is that card safe? Unless you know, it's simply a matter of luck to avoid the Old Maid.

Variations: Instead of removing a queen, randomly remove from the pack one card which no one sees. In this way, only at the very end will all the players discover which card in actuality was the "Old Maid."

For a quicker game, you can shrink the pack by omitting all cards of several ranks.

PANGUINGUE

Pan, a gambling game especially popular out West, can also be enjoyed

as a party game. It grew out of Coon Can and uses the same cards,

only lots more of them! It also has a language of its own.

Number of players: Up to 15, though best when limited to eight.

Objects: To meld certain groups of cards ("conditions"), and to be the first to "go out" (meld all cards).

The cards: Five or more Coon Can packs (regular packs of 52 cards with all 8s, 9s, and 10s omitted) are shuffled together. Aces are low.

To play: Unlike in other games, in Pan the deal and play rotate counterclockwise (to the right).

Deal ten cards to each player, in batches of five. Leave the remaining stock in the center of the table, turning its top card over to begin a discard pile.

Dropping: Each player decides whether to drop or play after looking at his hand. If you drop, throw in two chips. These chips will go to the winner of the hand. Dropping is also known as "going on top," because the forfeited cards are stacked on the foot of the stock. The discards don't belong to the stock and cannot be played.

If you decide to play, you must stay in until the end. The closest remaining player to dealer's right goes first. The object of play is to meld 11 cards. A meld must consist of at least three cards in a group or sequence. A sequence is any three cards of the same suit, in sequence; a group is three or more cards of the same rank.

At each turn, you may take the upcard if you can meld it or add it on to a meld you already have. Otherwise, draw the top card of the stock. After drawing, table any melds you may have, and discard one card.

There are two types of melds: payoff melds (conditions) and non-payoff melds. When you lay down a condition, each active player immediately pays you according to the following chart. Note that spades score double in all conditions.

All 3s, 5s, and 7s are "valle" cards, meaning they are cards that have value. Cards of any other rank ("square" cards) do not have value.

Any group of valle cards, different suits	1 chip
Any group of valle cards, same suit	2 chips
	(4 chips in spades)
Any group of non-valle cards, same suit	1 chip
	(2 chips in spades)
Any sequence of A-2-3	1 chip
	(2 chips in spades)
Any sequence of J-Q-K	1 chip
	(2 chips in spades)

Payoff melds (conditions)

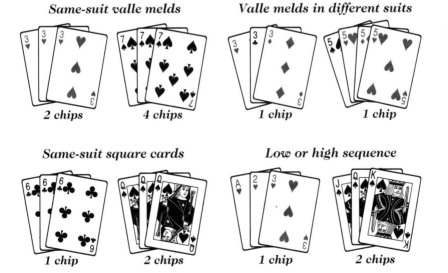

Same-suit valle melds

2 chips   4 chips

Valle melds in different suits

1 chip   1 chip

Same-suit square cards

1 chip   2 chips

Low or high sequence

1 chip   2 chips

Non-payoff melds

Sequence of three or more	Non-comoquers (kings and aces in groups of three or more, any suits)

Other square cards, must be three different suits

Groups of three or more square cards must be three different suits. With three different suits, however, you can lay off any duplicates at that time as well.

Sequences must be either low or high; for example, ♥K-♥A-♥2 is not a valid meld. ♣5-♦6-♠7 is not a valid meld either, because a sequence must be all of the same suit.

Laying off cards: You may lay off cards onto your own melds, but not onto other players' melds. Whenever you lay off an additional card on a pay spread, you are paid again by each player. Exception: Payment for extending a same-suit valle card spread pays half—just 1 chip, and 2 in spades.

Switching: You can rearrange or switch your own melds in two ways: You can take the fourth of a group and use it in another meld, and you can reshape sequence melds.

Special terms in Pan:

Condition. A spread that pays to its owner.

Going on top. Dropping out before play starts.

Non-comoquers. All kings and aces.

Rope. A sequential meld.

Spread. Any meld.

Square cards. As, 2s, 4s, 6s, Js, Qs, Ks.

Valle cards. 3s, 5s, 7s.

By taking the ♥6 (the fourth card from the meld) and adding it to the ♥5 and ♥7 from your hand, you form a "rope."

Here, the cards have been rearranged to form a condition in spades! Collect 2 chips from every player.

Forcing: If at your turn the top discard can be laid off onto your melds, you are not obliged to take it unless another player demands that you do. This is called forcing. Upon adding the card to your meld, you must then discard.

Scoring: Whoever goes out first is the winner. Winner receives 1 chip from every player who did not drop, plus additional payment for all his conditions. In effect, then, the winner is paid twice for his payoff melds.

Tips: The most important decision is whether to play a hand or pay the penalty and "go on top." Usually you should stay in a hand if it contains valle cards and others that may give you pay spreads. You should also stay in the game if your cards work together and your hand offers good possibilities of melding.

Variations: Panguingue houses often use a special pack. From eight Coon Can packs, one suit of spades is omitted, leaving 310 cards. Sometimes an extra ♠3, ♠5, ♠7, ♠2, and ♠Q are also removed. In such games, the player with the lowest card receives the first deal, and thereafter the winner of each deal receives cards first.

PIQUET

---◆◇◆---

Piquet is over 550 years old! Legend says it was invented by a knight who fought with Joan of Arc. In 1743, Piquet was one of five games covered in a treatise on games. Packed with French verbiage, Piquet has flourished in England, where it's pronounced "picket."

---◆◇◆---

Number of players: Two.

Object: To outscore your opponent over six deals (a "partie").

The cards: A pack of 32 cards is used. (Remove all 2s through 6s from a standard pack.) Aces are high.

To play: Deal 12 cards to each player and place the remaining eight cards in a face-down "talon." Nondealer may then choose to discard at least one and not more than five cards in exchange for an equal number of cards from the top of the talon. If nondealer exchanges fewer than five cards, he may peek at those he did not take. Dealer may then exchange for as many cards as nondealer has left behind. The goal of both players in this exchange is to form scoring combinations (see "Declaring").

Nondealer discards ♠7, ♦9, and ♦8 and takes the top three talon cards. Since nondealer discarded only three cards, he may peek at the next two talon cards and put them back in place.

Carte blanche: When you're dealt no picture cards, you have "carte blanche." Before the exchange, show your hand to your opponent and score 10 points.

Declaring: After the card exchanges, the players determine who has the better scoring combinations in three categories: point, sequence, and sets, in that order.

Point. The suit with the highest point count (aces count 11, face cards 10, and pip cards their face value). For example, dealer's ♠A-♠Q-♠J-♠10-♠8 (49) beats nondealer's ♦A-♦K-♦Q-♦9-♦8 (48), for a score of 5 (1 per card).

Sequence. The longest sequence in a single suit (minimum three cards). If players have sequences of the same length, the one headed by the higher card wins. A sequence of three cards (a "tierce") scores 3. A sequence of four (a "quart") scores 4. A sequence of five or more scores the number of cards plus 10.

Sets. Sets of three or four cards of the same rank. A player with a foursome (a "quatorze")—for instance, ♦Q-♥Q-♣Q-♠Q—beats a threesome (a "trio")—♠A-♣A-♥A—regardless of rank; but in sets the same size, then the highest rank scores. Trios score 3 and quatorzes 14.

Nondealer begins the dialogue, starting with point. In the example given, nondealer would say "48" to which dealer would say, "Not good, 49." In each group, only the player with the winning meld scores. That player may also score for all other qualifying melds in that category. If players tie for best in a category, neither scores. For strategic reasons, you may choose not to declare a meld. This is called "sinking the meld."

The play: Play to 12 tricks with no trump. Nondealer leads any card to the first trick. The highest card of the suit led wins the trick, and the winner of a trick plays to the next. In the play, score 1 point for every trick you lead to, and 1 for every trick opponent leads that you win. For example, if nondealer wins the first two tricks but loses the third, nondealer has still scored the first 3 points of play, which can be significant in the scoring. The winner of the last trick scores 1 bonus point. Whoever wins more tricks scores a 10-point bonus, but if one player wins all 12 tricks, called a "capot," the bonus is 40 points. Thus, if you lead and win all 12 tricks, you score 53 (12 for the leads, 1 for last trick, and 40 for capot).

Nondealer   Dealer

Dealer has a great-looking hand, but nondealer's is even better. (Nondealer's hand is the same one as illustrated on page 58 after the three exchange cards: ♥Q-♥9-♠9.) Nondealer's point is a seven-card suit (♥A-♥K-♥Q-♥J-♥10-♥9-♥8) with a higher count than dealer's (♣A-♣K-♣Q-♣10-♣9-♣8-♣7). Nondealer scores 7 for point. Nondealer's seven-card sequence is worth 17, and his three-card sequence (♠J-♠10-♠9) is worth 3: Nondealer scores 20 in sequences. Nondealer also has a group of four (♥J-♠J-♣J-♦J), which beats dealer's trios (aces, kings): Nondealer scores 14 for this quatorze. Dealer, beaten in every category, does not score at all!

In the illustrated hand, nondealer would likely take the first seven tricks and score 8 points (1 point per lead). Dealer would take the last five tricks and score 6 points, including 1 for last trick.

Scoring: If you score the first 30 (or more) points of a hand, you score either the "pique" or "repique" bonus.

Repique bonus (60 points): If either player scores 30 or more points just in card combinations before opponent scores any, he wins the 60-point repique bonus. In the hand shown, nondealer scores the first 41 points in card melds, earning 60 points more for repique.

Pique bonus (30 points): If nondealer scores the first 30 points in card combinations and trick-taking, he earns a 30-point bonus for pique. Dealer cannot win pique, because nondealer automatically scores 1 for leading.

By custom, players announce their running totals throughout the hand, writing scores down at the end. Deal alternates, with six deals constituting a Piquet "partie," or game. At the end of the partie, if both players have more than 100 points, the winner gets the difference in scores, plus a 100-point game bonus. However, if the loser has under 100 points, the winner, regardless of score, gets both scores combined, as well as the 100-point game bonus. The loser is said to be rubiconned, having not crossed the "rubicon" of 100 points.

Tip: In play, much depends on who leads first. Take a look at the hand shown. Switch the players' seats and dealer would take every trick, if only dealer could go first! This rule affects your card-exchanging strategy. Dealer may need to keep strength in each suit to avoid giving up a capot. On the other hand, nondealer can discard all cards of a suit, to increase the chance of a capot.

Variation: Instead of playing a Piquet partie, play *Piquet au Cent,* in which the game ends as soon as one player reaches 100 points.

POKER

---◆---

Poker has endless variants, but they fall into three main groups: Draw Poker, Stud Poker, and Hold 'Em Poker. The standard poker game rewards the best (highest) hand, but there are numerous forms of Lowball Poker where the worst hand wins. In recent years, there's been a surge of High-Low Poker, where the best hand and the worst hand get to divide the same pot. Many poker sessions are "dealer's choice," where the dealer picks from a bunch of games the players know.

---◆---

Object: To win the pot, either by being the only player left or by having the best cards.

General Poker rules:
- Each player receives a stack or stacks of chips.
- Deal and betting proceed clockwise (to the left).
- At the showdown (end of the hand) the last to bet—or to raise the bet—shows first.
- Players calling the final bet have a right to see the cards of all others who call.
- If at any point only one player is left, that hand wins and need not be shown.

Rank of hands in Poker:
Royal flush: Five sequential cards of the same suit to the ace. (♥10-♥J-♥Q-♥K-♥A)
Straight flush: Any five sequential cards of the same suit. (♥7-♥8-♥9-♥10-♥J)
Four of a kind: All four cards of a rank. (♣6-♥6-♦6-♠6)
Full house: Three of a kind plus a pair. (♥3-♠3-♣3-♦10-♠10)

Flush: Any five cards of a suit. (♠Q-♠9-♠8-♠5-♠2)

Straight: Five cards in sequence, any suits. Note that ace can be either high or low. (♦A-♥2-♣3-♦4-♠5)

Three of a kind: Three cards of one rank, the rest unmatched. (♠K-♦K-♥K-♣9-♦7)

Two pair: Two different pairs of two cards of a rank, the rest unmatched. (♦J-♣J-♥8-♣8-♥5)

One pair: Two cards of a rank, the rest unmatched. (♦J-♣J-♥8-♣7-♥5)

High card: No combination. Aces are high. (♣A-♠7-♥9-♣10-♣4)

Between hands of the same type, the higher-ranked hand wins. For example, a flush headed by a jack (♣J-♣9-♣5-♣3-♣2) beats a flush to the 10 (♦10-♦9-♦8-♦5-♦3); queens up (♥Q-♦Q-♣3-♠3-♥4) beats 9s up (♠9-♥9-♣8-♥8-♠K).

Wild cards: In some games, dealer may call certain cards "wild"—that is, they can stand for any other card. Sometimes a joker is added as a wild card. Deuces wild (all four of them) is another popular choice. Another favorite is "One-eyes wild" (the three face cards in profile: ♦K, ♥J, and ♠J).

Lowball Poker: Lowball Poker can be played in as many styles as "high only" poker. There is usually a round of betting, a draw, then another betting round and a showdown. Aces rank low. The hand that ranks as the poorest poker hand wins. For example, ♠7-♣3-♥9-♦4-♣5 (a 9-low) beats ♥4-♣A-♦2-♠J-♥3 (a jack-low).

Most lowball versions disregard flushes and straights and pay attention only to the number value of the cards, so that 7-6-5-4-3 is a 7-low. (Make very sure that all players are clear on this.) When hands competing for low have the same worst cards, look to the next worst card. For example, 8-5-4-2-A beats 8-6-3-2-A.

High-Low Poker: In High-Low Poker, the best hand and the worst hand divide the pot. Any form of poker—Draw, Stud, or Hold 'Em—can be played High-Low. High-Low differs from one-winner poker games in several important ways.

General terms in Poker:

Ante. An initial stake each player puts in.

Betting in the blind. Betting without seeing your cards.

Bluffing. Betting or raising with a weak hand.

Broadway. A straight to the ace.

Call. To equal a bet made by another player.

Check. To pass.

Drop. To quit a hand.

Fold. To quit a hand.

(the) Goods. A real hand, no bluff.

Hole cards. In stud poker, face-down cards.

Openers. A good enough card combination to meet a minimum requirement.

Pat hand. A hand you don't draw to.

Pot. All the bets in the center of the table.

Pot limit. A dangerous game, where the bet limit is the sum of chips in the pot.

Raise. To equal another's bet and add to it.

Sandbag. To check (pass), and later raise in the same round.

See a bet. To equal it, call.

Sixth street. The last upcard in seven-card stud, before a downcard is dealt.

Stand pat. Draw no cards.

Trips. Three of a kind.

Wheel. A hand good for both "high" and "low."

The declaration: In most games, players declare, before the showdown, whether they are going "high," "low," or "high and low." In some games, this is done out loud, by going around the table starting with the last raiser or bettor. This reduces some surprises and gives a certain positional advantage for which to play.

A more common practice is to declare silently, but at the same time. This can be done using chips or coins. At a signal, players either put no chips in their hand to go low, one chip in their hand to go high, or two chips to go high and low. In some games, this is the final action, after which the winners and losers are sorted out. In some games these declarations are followed by one more betting round (the "drive") that gives bluffers and legitimate hands one more chance to raise the pot. Since one player may have a lock on half the pot, High-Low poker limits raises to three per round.

Most High-Low games encourage you to go for high and low on the same deal, if you've got the right hand. This is easy in seven-card games, where you can use different sets of cards for each direction you go. In five-card games, it must be clear whether a 2-3-4-5-6 straight can be low, that is, a "6-low." If you go high-low but lose in either direction (high or low), you're out of the hand.

In any kind of poker, it's important that all players know the bet limits and the rules and agree to the games being played.

DRAW POKER

Number of players: Two to seven.

The cards: A regular pack of 52 cards is used.

To play: Each player antes one chip. Cards are dealt one by one until each player has five. The first player then may bet or check, but once a player has bet, each player in turn either folds or sees the bet (and perhaps raises it).

Once all bets and raises have been called, the dealer proceeds to ask each player in turn how many cards they wish to draw. The maximum number of cards a player can draw is three. Each player casts unwanted cards aside, and the dealer deals replacements. Dealer's own draw should be clearly announced, for example, the dealer may state, "Dealer takes two." A player who draws no cards is said to "stand pat."

Once players have all received their new cards, the final round of betting takes place, beginning with the player who made the last raise or bet. Most games establish a betting limit, which on the second round is usually double the first.

When all bets and raises have again been called, there is a showdown to see whose hand is best. Usually the last bettor shows first, and others may choose to fold their hands if beaten. However, the remaining players in the pot have a right to see all hands that have called.

If all players pass on the first round, throw the hand in. The deal passes to the left, and another round of five cards is dealt. Leave the chips in the pot, as players add another ante.

Tips: Most fairly serious poker games should have house rules that all players know in advance of play. For example, many games limit the number of raises in a round to three, unless only two players remain, who can then raise and re-raise each other as they wish. Other matters to clarify ahead of time include misdeals, misstatements of hands, maximum bets, and buying new chips, among others.

Variation: In *Jacks or Better,* the player who makes the first bet (the "opener") must have a pair of jacks or higher. These openers must be shown if asked later in the hand. If no one has an opener, each player re-antes for a new deal. In this way, the pot grows if no one can open. Some play that "progressive" openers are needed on each next hand: queens, then kings, then aces, then two pair, then back to aces, and so on.

HOLD 'EM POKER

Number of players: Two to ten.

Object: To join your two cards with any three on the table to make the best hand.

The cards: A regular pack of 52 cards is used.

To play: After each player antes, deal two cards face down to each player and five cards face down in the center of the table. Starting with the player at dealer's left, each player may check or bet. Once a player has made a bet, subsequent players must fold unless they see—or raise—the bet.

Once all first-round bets are called, the dealer turns over the first three face-down cards. These are called the "flop." You must use both your hole cards with three from the table to form the best possible hand.

Whoever was the last bettor starts a new round of betting, after which the dealer turns up one more card from the center of the table. Another betting round ensues, and then the dealer turns over the last card for a final betting round. Whoever has the best hand and is still in the betting wins the pot.

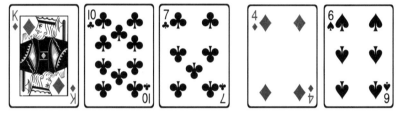

The three cards on the left make up the flop.

Tips: This is a game with no surefire advice, for each hand is different, and many different factors affect what the other players do. Some combinations, such as ♣K-♣Q, may seem to have greater prospects than ♦2-♠7, but if the flop is ♥7-♥2-♦7, you'd rather have the second hand. By betting on the first round with ♣K-♣Q, however, the ♦2-♠7 might drop before the flop.

Variations: Many varieties of Hold 'Em exist, and new ones are constantly being invented. One popular alternative is to deal players three cards rather than two. In this version, players choose two cards of the three from their hands to use, along with any three on the table. This makes the average winning hand a better one.

A popular practice is to require the first hand to toss in a bet "in the blind" (without seeing their cards), and the second hand then to follow with a "raise in the blind." The next players may drop, call, or raise. This invites players to call with moderate cards.

Stud Poker

Number of players: Two to eight.

The cards: A regular pack of 52 cards is used.

To play: In five-card stud poker, each player antes. Deal one card down and one up to each player, as shown below.

Dealer

The ♣K is the high card. This player may check or bet. If ♣K bets, then the player with the ♥10 sees the bet, or else drops (shown by turning the ♥10 over), and so on with each player around the table. Since the ♣K was dealt first, it has betting priority over the ♥K.

The player with the highest card showing starts by checking or by betting. As soon as there's a bet, the players following must, in turn, either fold or call—and perhaps raise—the bet.

Once all bets are called, the remaining players each receive another upcard. Another round of betting follows, started by the player with the best hand showing.

Each round of cards dealt up is followed by a betting round. The final round of bets occurs when all players left in the hand have four upcards. This round of betting should have a higher limit than the previous rounds. Also, if any player shows a pair at any time, the bet limit is raised.

After the final bets, the bettor—or last raiser—is usually first to turn over the hole card. If no one calls the last bet or raise, the winner gathers the pot and isn't obliged to show anyone the winning hand.

You and one player remain from the hand dealt on page 68. You now show a pair of kings. Your opponent must have an ace in the hole to have any chance to win. If you have a king, 6, or 4 in the hole, you are a sure winner. Bet only as much as you think your opponent might call. If you are not a sure winner, however, you must decide what to do. In situations like this, a "poker face" is called for!

Variations: In seven-card stud poker, the mechanics work just as in five-card stud, except that two hole cards are dealt before the first upcard. After a fourth upcard is dealt to each player, the next card is again dealt down, in the hole. After this, one more betting round ensues.

Anytime a pair is showing, a higher bet limit applies. After the sixth and seventh cards, the higher bet limit also applies. To decide the pot, players use their best five cards out of the seven cards dealt.

RUMMY

Rummy originated in the camps and saloons of the old West, where it was known as Whiskey Poker because it was played for drinks. As times changed, so did the game. It received many new names and traveled in many directions, leaving favorite versions all around. Every Rummy game has its own appeal.

Back in the 1930s, Gin was a minor branch of the Rummy family tree, just becoming known, when suddenly it was embraced by all the Hollywood stars. This link to the cinema's elite quickly turned Gin Rummy into a national craze. It remains one of the all-time-best two-handed games.

One of the interesting parts of Old-Fashioned Rummy—also known as Straight Rummy—is that although you cannot knock, you do have plenty of opportunities to lay cards off. 500 Rummy, a topsy-turvy type of Rummy, has also been called Pinochle Rum and Michigan Rum. In this version, everyone gets points for melds, and instead of trying to go out, you try to stay in and rack up a higher and higher score.

Melds in all Rummy games: Melds in Rummy consist of groups of three or more cards of the same rank or sequences of three or more cards in one suit.

Sample melds in Rummy.

GIN RUMMY

Number of players: Two or three, or four can play as partners.

Object: To meld your cards, and score for "Gin" or "Knock."

The cards: A regular pack of 52 cards is used. Aces are low.

To play: Deal ten cards to each player. Turn one card up—the "knock" card—to begin a discard pile, placing the remaining cards face down next to it as a draw pile.

Nondealer may take the knock card and discard. If nondealer declines the knock card, dealer may take it and discard. Should neither player want it, nondealer draws the top card from stock and discards.

Turns alternate. At each play, take either the top discard or the top card from stock and then discard. Look to match cards in your hand into melds. When all your cards are melded, call "Gin" (or "Gin Rummy"), discard face down, and show your hand.

Melds in Gin

Groups of three or four cards of the same rank.

Sequences of three or more consecutive cards in one suit. Aces are low only.

Knocking: If you wish to stop the round before you or your opponent reaches gin, you may knock. Simply discard face down and say "Knock." Or, simply rap the table. Put down your melds, setting aside your unmatched cards—called "deadwood." Your total deadwood count must not be greater than the original knock card (see "Scoring" for card values). If the knock card was ♦8 and you have ♣10-♣J-♣Q-♣K, ♠9-♣9-♥9, ♦A, ♠2, ♣4, your deadwood cards offer little melding hope. Since their count totals only 7, however, you should knock.

Laying off: After a player knocks, opponent has the opportunity to "lay off" any possible melds onto the tabled melds. In this way, opponent can reduce his point total (see "Scoring"). Laying off is not permitted after a gin.

Scoring: Unmelded picture cards count 10, and all others their pip value (aces count 1). If you gin, score your opponent's deadwood total, plus a 25-point bonus. If you knock, score the difference between your knock-count and opponent's remaining deadwood cards after making any layoffs.

As sometimes happens—especially after laying off—your knock count may be greater than your opponent's deadwood. In this case, opponent scores the difference in count, if any, plus a 20-point bonus for the underknock (also called "undercut"). If your opponent lays off every unmelded card, the bonus is 25 points for "ginning off."

Should neither player make gin or knock, the hand is thrown in. Common practice is to stop play when two talon cards are still left. Game is generally played to 100 points.

Tips: Gin is a good game for memory-training: It will pay to recall which cards have already been played, especially the ones taken by your opponent. Be aware, however, that your opponent will also notice the discards you pick up!

A few helpful "don'ts":
- Don't pick up a discard unless it gives you a meld, or unless you have a very poor hand and your pick opens up a few chances. An exception might be to pick up a low-count discard (an ace or deuce) when you have a bad hand and a safe discard to make.

- Don't hold on to a high melding chance that only one card can fill. For instance, don't hold on to ♦10- ♦Q if you can draw any better or lower cards.
- Don't expect to find a third ace when you have two, unless you get lucky and draw it from the talon. That's not a card your opponent would discard except with a very good hand.
- Don't play for gin when you can knock early.

Variations: When the upcard turned is an ace, it's a common practice to play the hand for gin—knocking isn't allowed. Many people play that you count the hand double if the upcard is a spade. Another custom is for nondealer to receive an eleventh card, with no upcard turned. Play begins with nondealer's discard. You may knock any time your deadwood count is 10 or less.

In *Three-Handed Gin Rummy,* it's more difficult to reach a Gin hand, unless you allow both opponents a shot at the discard.

KNOCK RUMMY

Number of players: Two to five is best, but six may play.

Object: To knock when you have a lower deadwood count than any of your opponents.

The cards: A regular pack of 52 cards is used. Aces are low.

To play: For two players, deal ten cards each. For three or four players, deal seven cards each. With five or six players, deal just six cards each, leaving enough cards for each player to have several turns.

Knock Rummy proceeds like Gin Rummy, with two major differences. The first difference is that you may knock on any turn, with any deadwood count, and the second is that no cards are laid off on the knocker's melds.

As the play rotates, the discard is available only to the player whose turn it currently is.

Scoring: When someone knocks, show your cards, separating melded combinations from deadwood. Whoever has the lowest deadwood count wins the difference from each other player. If you knock and are tied, the player you tie with is deemed the winner, and collects from the others. When you knock and do not have the lowest hand, pay an extra 10 points to the winner of the hand.

When you knock with a fully melded hand ("going rummy"), you win a 25-point bonus from each player, in addition to their deadwood counts.

Tips: With two players, if you're dealt a deadwood count in the 40s, that may often be lower than your opponent's count. Since losing costs an additional 10-point penalty, however, you should probably make a quick knock only if under 35.

With more players, the added bonus for "going rummy" may influence you to play out a hand with an early meld. That's okay if your deadwood cards are relatively high (7s and above) or if your unmelded cards have a good chance of making a meld. But if your deadwood count is low, you should end the round as early as possible—before your opponents draw enough lucky cards to win.

OLD-FASHIONED RUMMY
(STRAIGHT RUMMY)

Number of players: Two to six.

Object: To get rid of all your cards by melding and by laying cards off onto others' melds.

The cards: A regular pack of 52 cards is used. Aces are low.

To play: For five or six players, deal six cards each. For two, three, or four players, deal six cards or seven cards each.

Turn one card up to begin the discard pile. Starting with the player at dealer's left, either take the top discard or draw the top card from the stock. Before discarding, you may table melds or lay off cards on other melds.

The game ends when someone has melded or laid off every card from their hand. A final discard is not required. If no one can go out, and you've gone through the discard pile a second time, the hand is thrown in.

Scoring: Each hand is scored independently. Winner scores for all cards still held in players' hands, whether in melds or not. If you go rummy—go out on one play—you win double.

Tip: While melding gives your opponents chances to lay off cards, if you hold on to melds too long, someone may go out. Your melds will then turn into penalty cards.

---

500 RUMMY

Number of players: Two to eight, but three to five work best.

Object: To score points for melds and to meld all your cards.

The cards: For two to four players, a regular pack of 52 cards is used. For five or more players, use two packs of 52 cards. Aces are high or low.

To play: For two players, deal ten cards each; for more players, deal seven cards each.

Melds score according to the cards they contain: High aces count 15; low aces 1; face cards 10; all others their pip value.

The use of the discard pack is unusual. In other Rummy games, the discard pile is a tight stack, with only its top card in view. Here, the discard pile is spread out so that all cards are in view.

Play starts at dealer's left, and at your turn you may take the top card from stock, or you can take any card in the discard pile—not just the top discard—as long as you use it as part of a meld. You also have to take all cards above the discard you take. Usually this is helpful, since your goal is to meld many points.

Besides making melds, you can also lay cards off on your own or others' melds. Since you'll be tallying your melds at the end of the hand, keep layoffs on others' melds within your own melding area.

Players keep cards laid off on sequence melds nearby, for scoring later. In this case, the ♣5 and ♣6 have been laid off on another player's ♣2-♣3-♣4 sequence.

The game ends when any player "goes out"—melds or lays off every card, with or without a final discard. No further melds, plays, or discards may occur. If no player should go out, the game ends when the entire stock is exhausted.

Scoring: At the end of play, total your melded cards, then subtract the count of cards left in your hand (whether meldable or not). Record each player's score. There is no added bonus for going out.

Tips: The strategy of 500 Rummy is nearly the opposite of other Rummy games. Keep high cards longer, because they're worth more. Since a discard can be available later, you may break up a low-scoring meld, allowing you to pick up more cards later. However, be careful when doing this, because someone else may have the same idea, and you could lose your card!

SCHAFKOPF

---◆◆◆---

Also spelled Schafskopf, this forerunner of Skat emphasizes skill in taking tricks. In the United States, it's often known by its translated name, Sheepshead.

---◆◆◆---

Number of players: Three. (Four or five players may sit at the table, with players taking turns sitting out.)

Object: To win at least 61 of 120 points available in tricks.

The cards: A 32-card pack, formed by omitting all 2s through 6s, is used. All queens, jacks, and diamonds are trumps. The plain suits—spades, clubs, and hearts—rank A (high)-10-K-9-8-7.

Ranking in order from left to right, these are Schafkopf's permanent trumps.

To play: The three players are called forehand (to dealer's left), middlehand, and endhand. Deal one round of three cards each, then two face-down cards—called the "skat"—that are set aside, a round of four cards, and another round of three cards, for a total of ten cards per player.

First, determine who will become the "Player" against the two others. Starting with forehand, either accept the role of Player by picking up the skat and then discarding two cards, or pass. If no one accepts, play the deal as a "Least" (see "Scoring").

No matter who is Player, forehand starts play by leading any card to the first trick. Always follow suit when able, but otherwise play any card. A trick is won by the highest trump in it, or, lacking any trumps, by the highest card of the suit led. Whoever wins a trick leads to the next until all ten tricks have been taken.

Cards count as follows:

Ace	11 points
Ten	10 points
King	4 points
Queen	3 points
Jack	2 points
7, 8, and 9	0 points

At the end of play, each side counts points taken in tricks. The Player must win at least 61 of the 120 points in play (including the two discards in the count). The Player's two opponents work together to win points and defeat the Player. Their chief strategy is to "smear" each other's tricks with high-scoring cards.

Scoring: Each player gains or loses game points as follows:

Points in play	Game points
61–90	2
91+ ("Schneider")	4
winning all tricks ("Schwarz")	6
31–60	−2
0–30	−4
winning no tricks	−6

When the hand is played at "Least," everyone tries to take as few points as possible. Whoever has the lowest total wins 2 game points, and a player taking no tricks scores 4 game points. If two players tie for least, whoever did not take the most recent trick (between the two) wins the 2 game points. If all three players tie at 40 points each, endhand scores the 2 game points. If you take all the tricks, you lose 4 game points.

The game ends when someone scores 10 game points.

This hand represents an excellent "take." You've got quite a few high trumps, though you're missing the highest one. You haven't seen the skat yet, but you can plan already on exchanging the ♣10, which will count in your tricks later. When you get the chance to trump a plain suit, use the ♦10 to be sure of winning it.

Tips: To help you remember the rank of queens and jacks as trumps, remember the word CaSHeD—Clubs, Spades, Hearts, Diamonds.

To accept, you almost certainly need more than your one-third share of the 14 trumps. But since you'll need to score points, it helps to have an ace or two.

Of the 120 points, 75 come from the aces, 10s, and kings of the plain suits, which have only six cards each. You can't count on everyone following even to the first lead. In fact, the Player's two discards very often create a "void" in at least one plain suit. As a defender, you may find that the way to win an ace is to be able to play it when your co-defender is winning a trick in another suit. Especially when you have very few trumps, look for chances to "smear"—to discard an ace or 10—on your side's trick.

Variation: In some games, a "Least" is played with no suit as trumps, with each suit ranked, from high to low, A-K-Q-J-10-9-8-7.

SETBACK

---◆◆◆---

*Setback is a quick game of trumps, filled with strategy and surprise.
Also known as Pitch and Auction Pitch, it is a descendent of the
Mississippi riverboat game Seven Up, where players keep track of
their points using a stack of seven chips.*

---◆◆◆---

Number of players: Three to five is best, but two to seven may play.

Object: To score points by winning high trump, low trump, jack of trumps, and "game."

The cards: A regular pack of 52 cards is used. Aces are high.

To play: Deal six cards each, in bunches of three. Starting at dealer's left, players each have one chance to pass or bid. A "bid" is a number—one through four—and must be a higher number than any earlier bid.

The high bidder—the "pitcher"—plays against everybody else. Four possible points can be won in play: "high" (the highest trump in play), "low" (the lowest trump in play), "jack" (the jack of trumps, not always in play), and "game" (the highest total of cards won in play). Aces count 4; kings 3; queens 2; jacks 1; and 10s 10.

The "pitcher" always begins play by leading a card. The suit led becomes trump. Because of this rule, you can silently bid four (the highest bid) simply by pitching a card to indicate your trump lead.

Always follow suit whenever possible. If unable to follow suit, play any card. Each trick is won by the highest trump it contains or, if it contains no trump, by the highest card of the suit led.

Although the defenders work together to set back the pitcher, they keep separate piles of the tricks they've each taken, since each independently scores any points earned.

In a four-player game, you win the bid at "Two," grateful that you didn't have to go "Three." You need to make any 2 of the 4 points. Here, "low" and "game" are the most likely points you'll win. Careful play should clear out your opponents' trumps, leaving an open path for your ♣2 to score the "low" point, and for you to win another trick with the ♦10.

Scoring: If you make your bid, score all the points you won. If you don't make your bid, you lose—or are "set back"—the number you bid. Regardless of how the pitcher fared, defenders score their individually won points.

Whoever reaches 7 points wins the game. When two players are near 7, always tally "high" point first, followed by "low," "jack," and "game."

Tips: A bid of one by the first player usually will not end the bidding, so you can often make this bid on a questionable hand to make the other players risk a bid of at least two.

An ace is always worth a bid of one, and it will often take two points, since the player with the lowest trump may have to play it. In the unusual case where just one trump is in play, it counts as both "high" and "low."

There aren't many cards in play besides the ones you see. In a three-handed game, only 12 other cards are out, in a four-handed game, it's 18. The outcome of most deals is therefore very unpredictable. However, the fewer cards out, the less likely it is that anyone will have the cards needed to set you back. For example, your king of trump will win the "high" point in a three-handed game nearly 75 percent of the time.

For a bid of four, you'll need to have the jack and win it, so your trumps need to be very good to make this bid safely. A hand like ♥A-♥Q-♥J-♥10-♣K-♣8 is likely to win four, but the bid carries a bit of risk if another player holds the ♥K and can capture the "low" point with it or, even less likely, the point for "jack." The low trump is probably easiest for you to win when it is in another player's hand.

Variation: Some credit "low" point to the player dealt the lowest trump instead of to the one winning it, but this leads to a less interesting game.

SOLO

This popular trick-taking game—a cousin of Whist—gives players a chance to form occasional temporary partnerships. Since you don't ever have to change seats in this informal game, Solo is well suited to a long trip.

Number of players: Four.

Object: To win enough tricks to fulfill your contract.

The cards: A regular pack of 52 cards is used. Aces are high.

To play: The turn to deal passes clockwise. Deal 13 cards to each player, turning dealer's last card up to specify a trump suit. The player at dealer's left, eldest hand, acts first. Eldest hand may pass or make one of the following calls, listed in rank from low to high:

Proposal (Prop): To take eight of 13 tricks with another player as partner.

Solo: To take five of 13 tricks playing alone against the three other players.

Misère (me-ZAIR): To take no tricks, playing alone with no suit as trumps.

Abondance (Abundance): To take nine of 13 tricks, playing alone against three opponents, with a suit other than the upcard as trumps. When this is the final call, announce the trump suit before the opening lead is made.

Misère Ouverte (me-ZAIR oo-VAIRT): To take no tricks, with no suit as trumps, and with the hand exposed on the table (also called "Spread").

Abondance in Trumps (Royal Abondance): To take nine of 13 tricks, with the upcard suit as trumps.

Abondance Declared: To take all 13 tricks against the other players, naming a suit as trumps.

You may only make a call if it outranks a prior call. For example, if a player has called Misère, you cannot then call Prop or Solo.

"Prop and Cop": A player proposes by saying "I propose" or simply "Prop." Any player who has not passed may accept the proposal, as long as a higher call has not been made. If you prop and no one accepts, you may convert your call into a higher one or else throw the hand in.

A player who passes cannot later make a call, except eldest player, who may accept a proposal after passing.

Regardless of who makes the final call, eldest hand leads to the first trick. One exception is at Abondance Declared, when the caller leads first. Dealer should remember to pick up the upcard before the second trick.

Players follow suit whenever possible, but otherwise may play any card. A trick is won by the highest trump it contains, or by the highest card of the suit led when it contains no trump. The winner of each trick leads to the next.

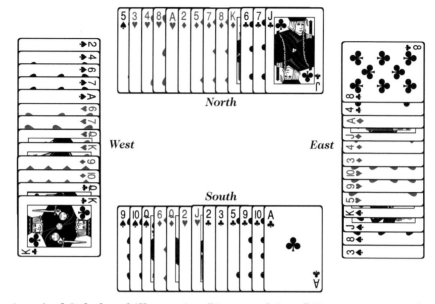

*A typical Solo hand illustrating "Prop and Cop." Hearts are turned
as trumps and West proposes with a good hand if joined by the right
partner. North accepts on a hand without many high cards, but
which will assist at hearts. East and South pass. West and North
become partners for the hand. They will probably take nine or ten
tricks together. West may start with the ♠A and then lead another
spade, which North will trump. This is a good beginning, as the partners are using their trumps one by one.*

Scoring: Each deal of Solo is scored independently. You may collect, or pay off, according to this typical scoring scale:

Prop and Cop	5 points
Solo	10 points
Misère	20 points
Abondance	30 points
Misère Ouverte	30 points
Royal Abondance	40 points
Abondance Declared	60 points

Tips: Hands scoring more than Misère don't come up that often,
but they are recognizable. An Abondance hand might be ♣A-♣K-
♣J-♣10-♣9-♣6-♦A-♦K-♦10-♦5-♦4-♠5-♥7. A Misère Ouverte
could be ♣A-♣10-♣6-♣5-♣3-♣2-♦J-♦7-♦4-♦3-♦2-♠4-♥3.

Most Solo hands will revolve around contracts of Prop and Cop. As the illustrated deal shows, you can take tricks with low cards if your side has the majority of trumps. In that deal, North seized the right opportunity to "Cop." Had North passed, East might have accepted West's prop, but this would be a closer battle for eight tricks.

Note that for Misère, you can't have any flaw: In the hand shown, North can be forced to win a heart trick or a club trick; South could be made to win a spade or a diamond at a Misère bid.

Variation: When all players pass, the hand is usually thrown in, but you may instead play a "grand," a no-trump contract where the winner of the final trick loses 10 points to each other player.

SPADES

It's curious that not much has been written about this widely known,

easy-to-learn trick-taking game. It's gathering new devotees from

within urban America, on college campuses, and even in cyberspace!

—◆—

Number of players: Four, playing as partners.

Object: To win the number of tricks bid by your side.

The cards: A regular pack of 52 cards is used. Aces are high.

To play: Partners sit opposite each other. Dealer deals 13 cards to each player. Spades are always trumps. There's one round of bidding, which starts at dealer's left. The first two players both bid the number of tricks—or "books"—they expect to take, while the second player in each partnership bids the total for the pair. For example, you deal, the player on your left bids four, your partner bids three, the next player bids five, and you bid seven. Your side has bid for seven tricks, your opponents have bid for five tricks.

There are several special bids that are optional in Spades.

10 for Two: A contract for ten books without a partner, with a two-to-one payoff.

Nil: A bid by the first bidder for a side for no tricks, which partner must convert to four tricks.

Blind Nil: Similar to Nil except the player may not look at the cards beforehand, though before play you and your partner may exchange one card. Your side must be down by 200 points to go for a bid of Blind Nil.

When you are dealt many spades and a pretty good hand, you might try "10 for Two" on your own. Save bids like seven and eight for hands that need your partner's help to reach ten books.

The player at dealer's left may lead any card other than a spade to the first trick. You must follow suit if able, otherwise you may play any card. A trick is won by the highest spade it contains or, if it contains no spade, by the highest card of the suit led wins it.

The winner of each trick leads to the next. Until a spade has been played on a non-spade lead, you can't lead spades unless all you have in your hand are spades. When you win a book, gather it in a packet that everyone can count with your other books.

Scoring: If your side makes its bid, score the bid number times 10, plus 1 for each extra trick, called a "sandbag." If your side fails to make at least the amount bid, you lose ten times the number of tricks bid. For example, your side bids seven, and your opponents bid five. You make nine tricks, while your opponents make four. Your side scores 72 points (7×10, plus two sandbags); opponents lose 50 (their bid, times 10).

If you succeed at 10 for Two, you win 200 points, but if you fail, you lose 100. For Nil, you win 100 or lose 100 as the case may be, but for Blind Nil you win 200 at the risk of 100.

Sandbags: When your sandbags total ten, subtract 100 points from your score (don't add 10). This works as a slow penalty for "underbidding" the number of books you take. Any leftover sandbags start a new count to ten.

Play until one side reaches 500 points, or any agreed upon count.

Tips: Because of sandbags, winning extra books is no help, so be on the lookout for a situation where you have both the high card and the low card in a suit and can control winning a book or losing it. If you have ♠10-♠7, for example, and you know that the only spade remaining is an opponent's ♠8, depending upon the number of tricks you want, you can choose whether to win the ♠8 or lose it.

Variations: In some games, the ♦2 is used as an extra trump, ranking between the ace and king. Some games add a joker for an extra trump and leave out a plain-suit deuce.

An interesting alternative to start the hand is for all players to put out their lowest club (or lowest diamond, lacking clubs) for the first book. The high club in this book wins it and leads to the next trick. With the first book played this way, the strategies for bidding and play are a little different.

Some Spades games allow a generous amount of informal chat between partners before deciding on their bid. You can say nearly anything except what cards you hold.

SPITE AND MALICE

Related to Russian Bank, this game has an ebb and flow, a give and take, and many shifts of pace. Because you can often regulate how much to do on one turn, you can make plays that annoy and frustrate your opponent. It has become a curious favorite of married couples.

Number of players: Two.

Object: To be the first player to get rid of all cards from your "payoff" pile.

The cards: Two packs of 52 cards are used, plus their four jokers. Aces are low. A joker can stand for any card except an ace.

To play: Players sit across from each other with a large playing area between them. Shuffle all four jokers with one of the decks; this creates a shared draw pile, placed face down between the two players. Shuffle and deal out the other deck card by card, giving each player a face-down 26-card payoff pile.

Players each turn up their top payoff card, leaving it face up on the pile. Whoever shows the lower card deals a five-card hand from the draw pile to each player. Nondealer plays first, turns alternating thereafter.

At each turn you are required to play any aces you have in your hand or on your payoff pile into the middle of the table. An ace begins a "center stack" that is built card by card up to king. Suit and color don't matter. Each available deuce is also required to be played onto a center stack whenever possible. If there is no ace in the center, you must wait to play the 2.

In addition, you may choose to make any, all, or none of other possible plays available:

- You can play one card from your hand to begin one of your four "side stacks" (start only one side stack per turn, until you have four). These side stacks give you a chance to organize your discards.
- You can play one or more cards from your hand onto one or more of your side stacks. Each card you add to a side stack, however, must be either the same rank as the topmost card showing, or one rank below it (any 9 on any 10, for instance). Each player can play only to his own side stacks, and only with cards from his hand. Color and suit don't matter.
- You can move the topmost card from one side stack either onto another side stack or to start a brand-new side stack (unless you already have four side stacks).
- You can play a card from your hand, your payoff pile, or your side stacks onto the center stacks. Play a 2 on an ace, a 3 on a 2, and so on upward to king. Suit and color don't matter.

Before beginning each turn, take cards from the draw pile to bring your hand back to five cards, replacing any cards you played on your last turn. Keep playing until you can't or choose not to make any further move. Just say "That's it," and your opponent takes his turn.

When a center stack is built up to the king, shuffle the cards from that stack back into the draw pile. You can wait for a few stacks to accumulate.

Bonus turns: Whenever you play all five cards from your hand in one turn, you get an extra turn. Take five new cards from the draw pile and keep playing.

When neither player can—or will—make a play, the game is blocked. In a blocked game, however, you must make any obvious plays your opponent requests in order to keep the game moving along.

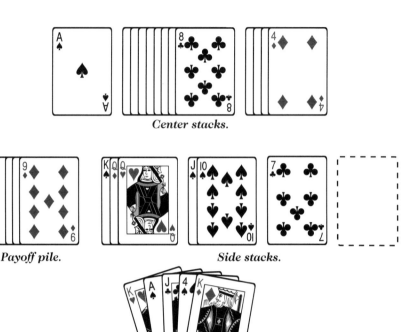

Center stacks.

Payoff pile.   Side stacks.

It's your turn. You must play ♠A to start a new center stack. You should also play ♦9 from your payoff pile on top of the ♣8 in the center, and follow with the ♠10, ♣J from your hand, then ♥Q-♥K. You may also begin your fourth side stack with ♦K. Since you have a new payoff card to turn up, you may still have plays left this turn.

Scoring: If you play out your entire payoff pile, you win a point for each card remaining in your opponent's payoff pile, plus a 10-point bonus. In a blocked game, whoever has fewer payoff-pile cards left scores the difference, with no bonus. Play to 25 points, or to any other agreed upon number.

Tips: Your immediate goal is always to reduce your payoff pile, so it is usually worth spending a joker or two—if need be—to play off your current payoff card. The next card you turn up may be easy to play off.

A constant goal is to make things difficult for your opponent. For instance, try to build center stacks just past the rank of opponent's current payoff-pile card.

Try to begin your side stacks with high cards, to give yourself chances to build downwards. Although you can play cards of the same rank on side stack cards, such piles are harder to empty. Sequential piles, however, play right off onto the center stacks.

Variations: Some versions let you play only one card in any turn to a side stack. Others follow the rule that layoffs in sequences must alternate between red and black cards.

TWENTY-ONE

Don't confuse this game with the casino game of Blackjack, also called

"21." Even children can play this easy-to-learn numbers game, and

anyone can win! It also offers a chance to practice counting skills.

Number of players: Two to seven.

Object: To win as many cards as possible, without going over 21.

The cards: A regular pack of 52 cards is used. Aces and picture cards count 1 point each, all others count their pip value.

To play: Deal the cards out equally, and set aside any remaining cards. Starting at dealer's left and continuing in a clockwise fashion, players build a card count up to 21. As each card is played, the new total is announced.

When you play a card that reaches 21 exactly, collect the cards in the center. However, when any card you have would go over 21, say "Stop." The player on your right collects the cards. The player who said "Stop," begins the next count toward 21.

The hand is over when the final player gathers in the last cards.

The count has gone 5-12-15-16-17-18. If you have a 3, you can score 21 exactly and win the cards. If you have an ace, deuce, or picture card, you can still play. Otherwise, say "Stop." The player on your right gathers in the cards, and you begin a new count.

Scoring: Players count the cards they've won, and each player's score is recorded. The first player to 50 points (or any other agreed upon total) wins.

Tip: A usual strategy for most players is to play their high-count cards early. This leads to more low cards in the later rounds, and so the center pile tends to be bigger after the first few builds to 21.

Variations: You can play this game "blind," where each player turns up a card from a pile at each turn, without knowing its value.

A similar game called *Twenty-Nine* is intended for partnership play. Deal 13 cards each. The player at dealer's left begins by playing any card, and players follow in turn, stating the new total with each card played. If you can't play without going past 29, you must pass. Whoever reaches 29 exactly wins the trick. The next player then begins a new count. Eight tricks are possible, although not always taken in play. The side with the most cards when no one can play to 29 exactly wins.

WAR

Along with Old Maid, War is one of the first card games we played as children. In practical terms, it rarely ends with a thorough defeat.

Number of players: Two or more.

Object: To win all the cards.

The cards: A regular pack of 52 cards is used. Aces are high.

To play: Divide the pack equally into a face-down pile for each player. At about the same time, each player turns over their top card. Whoever has the higher card wins both cards, and the process is repeated. Cards won may be placed on the bottom of your pack, or set aside until your pile runs down, at which point the cards taken must be played.

Occasionally, both players turn up cards of the same rank. This starts a "war," in which each player lays off three more cards face down, and then turns up the next card. Whoever's card is higher wins all the cards from that "war." If the cards are still tied, turn three more cards face down and then turn the next card up to determine the winner.

The game ends when one player has taken all the cards, but this can take a long time. You can try a shorter game, where you go through the cards just once or twice, and then see who has more cards. You may also decide to play until one player's hand is reduced to ten cards.

Tip: This is a game of sheer luck, so there is no advice to follow— just hope that you get most of the high cards!

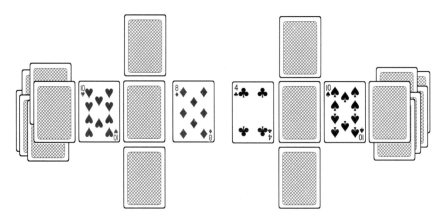

When there is a tie for high card, a war is waged to determine the winner. Here, players were tied at 10, and the player with the ♦8 is the winner of this war.

Variation: For three or more players, deal the cards out as equally as possible. Turn cards as before, and when players tie for best card, each plays two more face-down cards, with the next card turned up to decide a winner. Players not in the war must also contribute their next three cards. Play continues until one player has all the cards.

GLOSSARY

Bid. A spoken declaration to win a certain number of tricks or points; also, to make such a declaration.

Big Casino. In Casino, the ♦10.

Build. In Casino, to combine two or more cards so they can be taken with another card; also, the combination itself.

Canasta. In Canasta, a natural canasta is a meld of seven cards of the same rank. In a mixed canasta, from one to three cards are replaced by wild cards.

Contract. An agreement to win a certain number of tricks or points in a game or round.

Crib. In Cribbage, the extra hand, formed by the players' discards and belonging to the dealer.

Cutthroat. Each player playing on his or her own.

Deadwood. In Rummy games, cards in a player's hand that remain unmelded.

Deal. To give out cards before play.

Declaration. A statement to fulfill a contract.

Deuce. A card of the rank of 2.

Dix. In Pinochle, the 9 of trumps.

Draw. To take a new card or cards.

Draw trumps. To lead high trumps in order to deplete opponent's hand of trumps.

Face card. A king, queen, or jack.

Face value. The numerical value of a card.

Flush. A set of cards all of the same suit.

Follow suit. To play a card of the suit led.

Game. A total number of points to achieve; also, what constitutes winning or ending a game.

Gin. In Gin and Rummy games, a hand completely matched in melding sets, with no deadwood.

Going out. Playing, melding, or discarding your final card.

Hand. The cards a player holds; also, a deal of play.

Kitty. A common chip-pool; also (in a few games) cards available for exchange.

Knock. In Gin and Rummy games, to end play by laying down a hand that is not completely matched.

Lay off. To play one or more cards according to allowable plays.

Lead. To play the first card to a trick.

Left bower. In Euchre, the jack of the same color as the trump suit.

Little Casino. In Casino, the ♠2.

Marriage. A king and queen of the same suit.

Match. To equate by being of the same rank (or by another criterion).

Meld. A combination of cards with scoring value, generally three or more cards in sequence in one suit or all of the same rank; also, to show or play such a combination.

No-trump (no trump). The condition when no suit is trumps in a trick-taking game.

Pass. A spoken declaration not to make a bid; in Hearts, three hidden cards exchanged amongst the players.

Peg. In Cribbage, to score points.

Pip. A spade, heart, diamond, or club.

Plain card. Any 10, 9, 8, 7, 6, 5, 4, 3, 2, or ace.

Pot. A pile of chips or counters to be collected by the winner.

Right bower. In Euchre, the jack of the trump suit.

Sequence. Two or more cards in consecutive order.

Skunk. In Cribbage, to win by at least 30 points, or 60 in a game of 121.

Stock. The undealt cards available for future use.

Table. The playing area; also, to lay down a meld on the playing area.

Talon. A portion of the pack reserved for later use during the deal.

Trail. In Casino, to play a card to the table without building on or taking in other cards.

Trey. A card of the rank of 3.

Trick. A round of cards played, one by each player in turn.

Trump. A suit of cards designated to be higher-ranking than any other suit; also, to play a trump card on a trick.

Upcard. The first card turned up after a deal, often to begin play or initiate a discard pile.

Void. A lack of a suit in a player's hand.

Wild card. A card that can be designated by the holder to stand for any other card.